Study Guide

for

Modern International Economics
Second Edition

Study Guide

for

Modern International Economics
Second Edition

Wilfred J. Ethier
University of Pennsylvania

W • W • NORTON & COMPANY • NEW YORK • LONDON

W. W. Norton & Company, Inc. 500 Fifth Avenue, New York, N.Y. 10110
W. W. Norton & Company Ltd. 37 Great Russell Street, London WC1B 3NU

ISBN 0-393-95558-3

1 2 3 4 5 6 7 8 9 0

CONTENTS

Appendices

HOW TO USE THIS STUDY GUIDE

The International Economics course can seem a formidable one. The best way to study for it is with an aggressive, participatory approach to the subject: that is, read with pen and paper at hand, constantly asking yourself questions and working out the answers as you go along. This Study Guide encourages such participation.

You will find five main elements here, broken out to match the numbered subsections of each chapter in the text (except those subsections which are themselves applications, illustrations, or simple descriptions). First, the central points of each portion of the textbook are highlighted in a description of *Basic Ideas*. These are similar to the textbook's end-of-chapter summaries, but much more detailed.

Next, are the exercises themselves. There are four levels of exercises comprising hundreds of items—plenty of opportunity to practice. First come *Self-Tests*, for which the answers are provided at the end of the chapter, to give you a quick sense of whether you need more work on the material in a particular section. Next, you'll find *Solutions to Problems from the Text*, which provide answers for the problems in the textbook. Not *all* of the answers are given—a few are withheld for pedagogical purposes—nor is every answer meant to provide the last word in response to the question, but the answers provided should give you a clear sense of whether you have understood how to work the problems. Finally, *Additional Problems* are supplied here, of the same type as the *Solutions to Problems from the Text*, except that the answers are not supplied. In a separate section at the end of each chapter, a set of *Review Questions* will help you to pull together the entire chapter's material. Sample examinations— both midterms and finals—can be found in *Appendix B*. The best way to use these is to treat them like exams: give yourself the allotted time and do the best you can without text or notes. Then return to the text and to your notes to evaluate your answers and grade yourself.

PART ONE

The Pure Theory of International Trade and Its Application

CHAPTER 1   Comparative Advantage

1. The Simple Ricardian Model

Basic Ideas

1. The simple Ricardian model, which imagines that two countries can each produce two goods by means of a single productive factor, labor, is a useful way to understand the basic idea of comparative advantage.

2. According to comparative advantage, if labor is immobile between countries, each country should export the good which requires relatively less labor in its production than does the other good, compared to the other country, regardless of whether that other country can produce the good with absolutely less labor.

3. Definitions to know: **efficient pattern of production; opportunity cost; comparative advantage.**

Self-Test

1. True or false: A country should never produce a good in which it has a comparative *dis*advantage.

2. True or false: A country should never export a good in which it has a comparative *dis*advantage.

3. Multiple choice: The United States will have a comparative advantage in nothing:
   3.1. Indefinitely.
   3.2. If all labor requirements are low enough.
   3.3. If all labor requirements are high enough.
   3.4. Never.
   3.5. If labor becomes completely mobile internationally.

Solutions to Problems from the Text

1.1 *Suppose that in England five man-hours of labor are required to produce each cask of wine and five man-hours are required to produce each bolt of cloth, whereas in Portugal one man-hour of labor is required for a cask of wine and four man-hours for a bolt of cloth. (Except for the choice of numbers, this is the example used by Ricardo to discuss comparative advantage.)*

a. Who has a comparative advantage in what and why? Make two equivalent statements.

b. Prove that your answer to a is correct by showing in detail that when both countries are producing both goods, the world can be made better off by allowing England and Portugal to reallocate labor and trade in accordance with the pattern of comparative advantage. Derive the analog of Table 1.2 in the textbook.

c. Now suppose that it becomes possible to move labor between the two countries. What should be done?

a.   England has a comparative advantage over Portugal in cloth relative to wine. Portugal has a comparative advantage over England in wine relative to cloth.

b.   If England produces one less unit of wine and Portugal one fewer bolt of cloth:

	Additional Wine	Additional Cloth
in England	−1	+1
in Portugal	+4	−1
in World	+3	0

c.   All labor should be done in Portugal.

1.2   *In the context of the above problem, suppose that there is also a third country, France, where one man-hour of labor can produce either one bolt of cloth or one-half cask of wine. What statements can you make about comparative advantage? Which patterns of production and international trade are efficient?*

France has a comparative advantage over England and Portugal in cloth relative to wine. Portugal has a comparative advantage over England and France in wine relative to cloth. France should export cloth and Portugal should export wine; England's trade pattern cannot be prescribed without knowledge of tastes.

Additional Problems

1.   Given the data of Problem 1.1 above, what is the opportunity cost of wine in terms of cloth: in England? in the world if both countries are producing both goods? in the world if labor can be moved from country to country?

2.   Suppose that in Canada timber and steel each require 10 units of labor for the production of one unit of output, whereas in the United States 6 labor units can produce a unit of steel. What must be true of the U.S. labor requirements for timber production if: the United States is to have a comparative advantage in steel; the United States is to have

a comparative advantage in timber; Canada is to have a comparative advantage in steel; Canada is to have a comparative advantage in timber?

Answers to Self-Test

1. False

2. True

3. 3.4

2. Efficiency in the Simple Ricardian World

Basic Ideas

1. In the simple Ricardian model, the pattern of comparative advantage is revealed by a comparison of the slopes of two countries' production possibility frontiers.

2. An individual country will be on its production possibility frontier if its entire labor force is productively employed.

3. The world as a whole will be on its production possibility frontier if the entire labor force of each country is productively employed and if the pattern of production is consistent with comparative advantage.

4. Definitions to know: **production possibility frontier, marginal rate of transformation, productive efficiency.**

Self-Test

1. Multiple choice: Which of the following could cause a country's production possibility frontier to shift?
   1.1. A change in tastes.
   1.2. Growth of the labor force.
   1.3. A decrease in labor efficiency.
   1.4. A change in the pattern of production.
   1.5. The commencement of international trade.

2. True or false: A country has a comparative advantage in a good if its production possibility frontier is further from the origin than that of the rest of the world.

Solutions to Problems from the Text

1.4 *Consider, as in Problem 1.1, that in England five man-hours of labor are required to produce each unit of wine and each unit of cloth, while in Portugal one man-hour of labor produces one wine and four man-hours of labor produce one cloth. Suppose also that each country has 100 man-hours of labor available.*

a. *Draw the production possibility frontiers for England, Portugal, and the world. How do they change if England's labor force increases to 1,000?*

b. *If everyone in the world always consumes exactly one cask of wine for each bolt of cloth, what should each country produce and what should the direction of trade be?*

c. *Draw the world production possibility frontier if labor is internationally mobile.*

a.

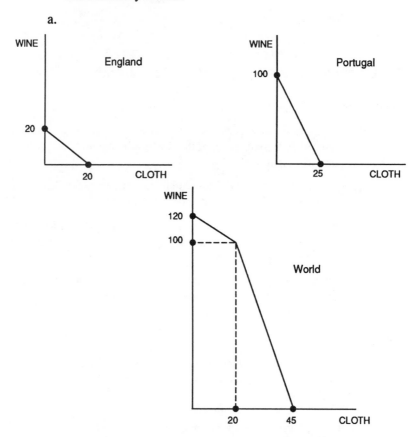

If England's labor force increases to 1,000, that country's frontier will shift out by a factor of 10 (as will its part of the world frontier).

b. England would produce 20 cloth and export 4 of it; Portugal would produce 16 cloth and 36 wine, exporting 16 of the latter.

c. Just like Portugal's frontier, but twice as far from the origin.

1.5 *In the above problem, suppose that in France one man-hour of labor can produce one cloth while two man-hours of labor are required for one wine, and, in addition, that France has 200 man-hours of labor. Draw the world production possibility frontier. Who is producing what at various points along it? Depict inefficient patterns of specialization.*

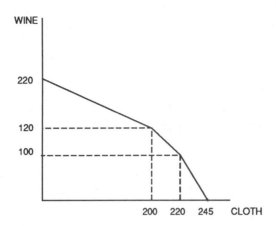

Additional Problem

Suppose that in Canada timber and steel each require 10 labor per unit of output, whereas in the United States 6 labor units can produce a unit of steel and 8 can produce a unit of timber. Canada has 1,000 labor units and the United States has 9,600. Draw production possibility frontiers for Canada, the United States, and the world. Describe what would happen if the world were to consume 400 timber and free trade were to take place.

Answers to Self-Test

1. 1.2 and 1.3

2. False

3. The Economics of the Simple Ricardian World

Basic Ideas

1. In equilibrium wages and prices must be such that, in each country, the price of a good equals its cost of production if that good is produced and is no greater than its cost of production if that good is not produced.

2. If two countries do not trade with each other, each will have a lower (autarky) relative price of the good in which it has a comparative advantage.

3. If two countries trade, their wage rates will adjust so that each can compete in the world market for the good in which that country has a comparative advantage.

Self-Test

1. True or false: A country with high wages cannot compete on world markets with countries where wages are low.

2. Give two reasons why a country might have low wages compared with its trading partners.

Solutions to Problems from the Text

1.6. *We have seen that the pattern of comparative advantage can be determined by comparing relative prices in the two countries when free trade is restricted. When the restriction is removed, trade proceeds according to comparative advantage, and prices in the two countries are driven toward common international prices. But if prices are the same everywhere, why should anyone bother to trade?*

Prices are the same everywhere because people trade.

1.7 *Suppose in the context of Table 1.1 of the text, that $w^F = 1$ and $w^G = 1$. Then both French prices are higher than both German prices, and, as we saw in section 3 of the text, international competition will cause the French wage to fall if the two countries trade. Does this not indicate that free trade will hurt the French worker?*

No, because the purchasing power of French wages does not fall.

1.8 *In Problem 1.4 (b), what will be traded and what will all prices be? Do both countries gain as a result of trade? By how much? If the world suddenly decides it will consume one cask of wine for every two bolts of cloth, how will your answers change?*

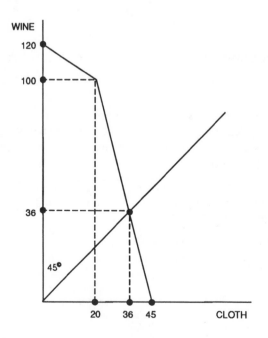

The world price $p = P_W/P_C = 1/4$ (Portugal's autarkic price). In Portugal, consumption consists of 20 units each of wine and cloth, the same as in autarky. England's consumption is 16 units of each, compared to 10 of each in autarky. England exports 4 cloth to Portugal in exchange for 16 wine, and England captures all of the gains from trade.

1.9 *The discussion in the text supposed that wages and prices in France and Germany adjusted themselves to each other entirely through inflation in Germany. Suppose instead that it happens entirely through French deflation, with German prices constant. Restate the argument in the text and write down the analog to Table 1.3.*

	Machines	Wine	Wages
France	6	2	2
France (after 50% deflation)	3	1	1/2
France (after 66% deflation)	2	2/3	1/3
France (after 83% deflation)	1	1/3	1/6
Germany	1	1	1

Additional Problem

If France and Germany engage in free trade, what can you say about their relative wage levels, w^F/w^G? Is this ratio determined by absolute cost differences or, like the pattern and the terms of trade, by relative cost differences?

Answers to Self-Test

1. False.

2. Because its labor is less efficient than the labor of its trading partners, and because world demand is low for the goods in which the country has a comparative advantage.

4. The Gains from Trade

Basic Ideas

1. International trade leaves each country at least as well off as in autarky, in the sense that the country can still afford to buy the goods it would have chosen if it were not trading.

2. The gains from trade are due to a difference between relative autarky prices and relative trading prices.

3. Definition to know: **terms of trade.**

Self-Test

1. Multiple choice: When we say that a country gains from international trade, we mean that
   1.1. Trade makes everyone in the country better off.
   1.2. The country as a whole consumes more of each good than it would without trade.
   1.3. Free international trade is better for a country than restricted international trade.
   1.4. All of the above.
   1.5. None of the above.

2. True or false: In the simple Ricardian model, trade between similar economies (in the sense of similar autarky price ratios) is unlikely to generate large gains for either country.

Solutions to Problems from the Text

1.11 *As in Problem 1.4, suppose that England has 100 man-hours of labor and requires 5 to produce each unit of wine and of cloth, whereas Portugal has 100 man-hours of labor, with 1 required to produce each unit of wine and 4 to produce each cloth unit. If the world relative price of wine in terms of cloth is one, what will be the pattern of trade and production; what will be the prices in each country; and who will gain from trade?*

If $p = 1$, the English autarkic price, Portugal must specialize in wine. Portugal exports wine to England for cloth, and all gains go to Portugal. If the English wage = 1, then $P_W = 5$ and $P_C = 5$ because England can compete in both markets. The Portuguese wage equals 5 because Portugal can compete in wine. Note that cloth costs 20 to make in Portugal, so that country cannot compete in that good.

1.15 *Suppose that when trade opens, France for some reason is forced to continue producing at point A in Figure 1.3 (a) of the text, instead of specializing in apples. How is the argument in the text altered? Compare this situation with both autarky and the case where France specializes.*

France would still be no worse off than in autarky, because she could still have A, and would now have alternative possibilities not available in autarky. But specialization would allow even better consumption possibilities:

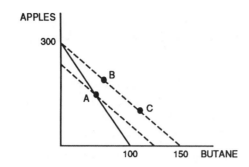

*1.16 *From 1792 to 1900, the United States was legally on a* bimetallic
standard: *the dollar was defined in terms of both gold and silver.
As a result of the Coinage Act of 1792, the U.S. mint stood
ready to convert gold and silver into coins, at the prices in the
first line of the table below, for anyone presenting either metal.
France was also on a bimetallic standard from 1803 to 1874, and
the bottom line contains hypothetical French prices illustrative
of the early part of this period.*

**Mint Prices of One Ounce of Gold and Silver,
Representative of 1804–1834**

	Gold	Silver
U.S.	$11.60	$ .77
France	fr60	fr3.87

*From the first line of the table, we see that the official U.S.
relative price of an ounce of gold in terms of silver was
$11.60/$.77 = 15 ounces. Similarly the French price of gold in
terms of silver was fr60/fr3.87 = 15.5 ounces.*

a. *Use the logical structure of the simple Ricardian model to
deduce what happened after passage of the 1792 act. France
was economically much larger than the United States in
those years.*

b. *The U.S. mint ratio was changed in 1834 and 1837 to about
16 silver ounces per gold ounce. The world price ratio by and
large remained near 15.5 to 1. What do you think happened
from 1834 to 1862 (the U.S. government abandoned metallic
standards during the Civil War)?*

a. Gold and silver are analogous to the two traded goods of the
simple Ricardian model, and the two national monetary units are
analogous to labor. Since France was the "large" country, the

equilibrium international price could have been expected to be 15.5 ounces of silver per gold. With U.S. authorities maintaining a price of 15, the United States could have been expected to "specialize" in, and export, gold. That is, any U.S. gold coins would have been melted down and exported to France where they could have been sold for more silver than they cost in the United States. Thus the U.S. money supply could be expected to consist only of silver coins. This is in fact what happened.

b. In this case the above argument is reversed. In fact, the U.S. money supply quickly came to consist only of gold coins, so that the country in effect switched from a silver standard to a gold standard.

Additional Problems

1. List all the reasons that you can think of for why a nation might actually be worse off as a result of international trade. Reconcile them with the theory you have studied.

2. We have studied how international trade is beneficial for a country as a whole, but there are always people within a country who think that trade is harmful to them. Try to explain this.

Answers to Self-Test

1. 1.5

2. True.

5. Unequal Exchange

Solutions to Problems from the Text

1.17 *Does your answer to Problem 1.11 show unequal exchange taking place?*

Yes, because the product of one hour of Portuguese labor exchanges for the product of five hours of English labor.

*1.18 *In the discussion of the simple Ricardian model, we were concerned with trade in commodities. But in a sense, the two countries were actually exchanging their labor services, because a unit of each good is actually an embodiment of the labor that produced it. This viewpoint came up in our discussion of unequal exchange. Define the "factoral terms of trade" to be the number of units of foreign labor a country can obtain by the sacrifice of one unit of domestic labor in this sense. What is the precise relation between the factoral terms of trade and the commodity terms of trade? What values can the factoral terms*

of trade possibly assume? What condition must the factoral
terms of trade satisfy for a country to gain by trade? Suppose
that France becomes more efficient in its export industries (say
a_A^F falls from 6 to 3) and thus exports more, causing the world
relative price p to rise. What will happen to the factoral terms
of trade? Which terms of trade do you think are a better index
of gains? Why?

Let f denote the French factoral terms of trade: $f = w^G/w^F$. Then,
assuming that France has a comparative advantage in apple
production,

$$p = f(a_B^G / a_A^F)$$

is the relation between the commodity and factoral terms of trade.
Thus

$$(a_A^F/a_A^G) \leq f \leq (a_B^F / a_B^G).$$

For France to gain from trade, f must be strictly less than the upper
bound. A fall in a_A^F and corresponding rise in p would leave f

unchanged, and in this case that would accurately reflect the effect on
French welfare.

6. Comparative Advantage in More General Circumstances

Basic Ideas

1. If we generalize the simple Ricardian model by abandoning the
    assumption that labor is the sole factor of production, the *MRT* and
    the autarky price ratio in a country are no longer determined simply
    by technology. Instead they become variables whose equilibrium
    values also depend upon tastes.

2. If the pattern of comparative advantage is deduced by a comparison of
    autarky relative prices (= *MRT*s), nearly all of our earlier conclusions
    remain valid.

3. The exceptions: the pattern of comparative advantage depends upon
    tastes as well as technology; it is no longer necessarily the case that
    with free trade at least one country must specialize completely in the
    production of a single good.

4. Concept to know: **increasing opportunity cost.**

Self-Test

1. Multiple choice: With free trade both countries will continue to
    produce both goods:
    1.1. Under no circumstances.

1.2. Always.

1.3. Only if there are in fact no gains from trade.

1.4. Whenever there are increasing opportunity costs.

1.5. None of the above.

2. In the simple Ricardian model, a country neither gained nor lost from trade if the free-trade relative price equalled that country's autarky relative price. Is this still true with increasing opportunity costs?

3. In the simple Ricardian model a country neither gained nor lost from trade if it produced both goods. Is this still true with increasing opportunity costs?

Solutions to Problems from the Text

1.19 *Recall that in section 1 of the textbook we considered the experiment of shifting labor from butane to apples in France and the reverse in Germany, recording the result in Table 1.2. Do the same now, in the context of increasing opportunity costs, and derive a table analogous to Table 1.2.*

	Additional Butane	Additional Apples
in France	− 1	French MRT
in Germany	+ 1	− German MRT
in World	0	French MRT − German MRT

*1.20 *Suppose that France exports apples to Germany in exchange for butane under increasing opportunity costs. Neither country is specialized. Now suppose that the cost of transporting one unit of butane from Germany to France equals 50 percent of the (German) cost of producing the butane. The cost of transporting apples, however, is so low that it can be ignored. What must be the free trade relationship between the prices of each good in the two countries? Suppose that a "transportation revolution" is expected to reduce by one-half the cost of shipping butane within the next four years. Can you predict anything about the likely effects of this on international trade and upon the pattern of production in both countries?*

(*Transportation Costs*) Let P_A^G denote the price of an apple sold in Germany. Competition will ensure that French and German apples sell for the same price in the same market. If P_A^F denotes the price of apples sold in France, international competition and the absence of a transportation cost for apples will ensure that $P_A^G = P_A^F$, that is, all apples will sell for a single world price regardless of where the apples

-14-

are produced or where they are sold. Denote this common price by P_W.

Similarly, within each market butane must sell for a single price regardless of where produced. But since there is a transportation cost to moving butane between markets, it need not sell for the same price in France as in Germany. As long as the price of butane in the two countries does not differ by more than this transportation cost, no one can make windfall profits simply by buying butane in the country with the lower price and then selling it in the country with the higher price. In this case we are told that the Germans export butane to France. Thus the price of butane in France must equal its price in Germany plus the transportation cost: $P_B^F = P_B^G (1 + 0.5)$.

Let p^F and p^G denote the relative price of butane in terms of apples in France and Germany respectively. Then $p^F = (1.5)p^G$ (Be sure that you can explain why!). That is, $p^F > p^G$. Then the principle of comparative advantage can be directly applied to conclude that the "transportation revolution" will cause Germany to shift production from apples towards butane, and to increase its exports of the latter, and it will cause France to do the reverse.

Additional Problems

1. Suppose that two countries are identical in size and technology, and so have identical production possibility frontiers. Is there any reason for them to trade with each other? Explain.

2. How does your answer to the previous problem change if the two countries also have identical tastes?

Answers to Self-Test

1. 1.5.

2. Yes.

3. No.

7. Tastes as a Determinant of Comparative Advantage

Basic Ideas

1. Each consumer's MRS will equal the relative commodity price prevailing in an economy, regardless of whether different individuals have quite different tastes or not.

2. Differences in MRSs across countries are a basis for mutually beneficial trade.

3. The principle of comparative advantage continues to apply to this trade, as long as the pattern of comparative advantage is defined on the basis of differences in relative autarky prices across countries.

4. Terms to understand: **production gain, consumption gain**.

*8. Exploring Further: Indifference Curves

Basic Ideas

1. An individual's tastes can be represented by a set of indifference curves, each connecting bundles of goods between which the individual is indifferent.

2. Under some circumstances the collective preferences of an entire society can be represented by a set of community indifference curves.

3. Such curves give a convenient geometric way to depict autarkic equilibrium and the gains from trade.

4. Term to understand: **community indifference curve**.

Solutions to Problems from the Text

1.21 *Prove that, for a single individual, two distinct indifference curves can never intersect.*

Suppose that two indifference curves did in fact intersect, as at point A in the diagram below. Since B and A are on the same indifference curve, the individual is indifferent between them. She must likewise be indifferent between C and A since they are also on the same indifference curve. Thus she must be indifferent between B and C. But this is not consistent with the two curves being distinct indifference curves.

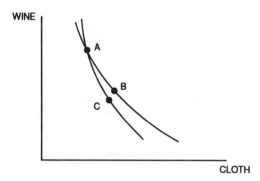

1.22 *Draw community indifference curves in Figure 1.7 of the textbook to show that international differences in tastes can serve as a basis for mutually beneficial trade.*

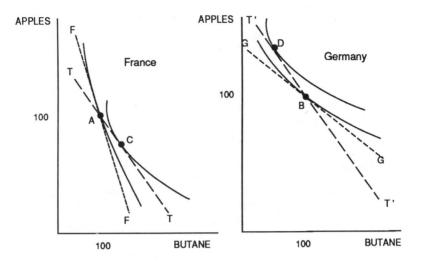

Additional Problems

1. Go through the discussion, in section 3 of the textbook, of the gains from trade, using indifference curves.

2. Draw the community indifference curves that depict the tastes described in Problem 1.4b: everyone always wants to consume equal numbers of bolts of cloth and casks of wine.

9. North-South Trade

Basic Ideas

1. Trade between the DCs and the LDCs is in basic accord with intuitive beliefs about the characteristics of those two groups of countries and the principle of comparative advantage.

2. There are nevertheless aspects of world trade which rest uneasily with comparative advantage, even though they are not logically incompatible with it.

3. These include the fact that the largest part of world trade is the exchange of manufactures between different DCs, and the large and growing share of intra-industry trade.

4. Terms to know: **intra-industry trade, inter-industry trade, product differentiation, division of labor, NICs.**

Self-Test

1. Multiple choice: The fastest growing part of world trade is:
   1.1 The export of manufactures from the DCs to the LDCs for primary products.

1.2. The exchange of manufactures among the DCs.

1.3. The exchange of primary products among the LDCs.

1.4. The export of manufactures from the LDCs.

1.5. Intra-industry trade among the DCs.

2. True or false: The principle of comparative advantage would seem to imply that intra-industry trade is not very important from a welfare point of view.

Solution to Problem from the Text

1.25 *Since the Second World War, the DCs have substantially lowered trade barriers, but the LDCs have not. Explain how Table 1.5 in the textbook seems to be consistent with comparative advantage. What would you expect to be true of the relative gains from the various trade flows, as distinct from their sizes?*

The principle of comparative advantage would lead us to expect proportionally more gains from trade between the DCs and LDCs, where comparative cost differences are greater.

Additional Problem

What practical difference does it make whether the actual pattern of world trade is explained by comparative advantage or not?

Answers to Self-Test

1. 1.4.

2. True.

10. Alternatives to Comparative Advantage: Scale Economies

Basic Ideas

1. Economies of scale furnish a basis for trade, quite distinct from comparative advantage, in which the pattern of specialization is unimportant: what matters is that countries specialize in something.

2. Increasing returns to scale help make the pattern of international trade indeterminate.

3. If trade is due to economies of scale, it is conceivable that a single country could be worse off than in autarky.

4. Scale economies may be either internal to the individual firm or external to it.

5. Scale economies that are internal to the individual firm are not consistent with a perfectly competitive industry.

6. Terms to know: **increasing returns to scale, decreasing returns to scale, internal economies, external economies.**

Self-Test

1. Multiple choice: Which of the following is an example of increasing returns to scale?
   1.1. Labor becomes more productive as more capital is invested in an industry.
   1.2. A new invention makes labor more productive.
   1.3. Existing plants become more productive as new firms enter the industry.
   1.4. All of the above.
   1.5. None of the above.

2. Multiple choice: Which of the following is an example of external economies?
   1.1. Labor becomes more productive as more capital is invested in an industry.
   1.2. A new invention makes labor more productive.
   1.3. Existing plants become more productive as new firms enter the industry.
   1.4 All of the above.
   1.5 None of the above.

Solutions to Problems from the Text

1.29 *If France has 10 labor units, and if Table 1.10 in the text describes the technology of both the apple and butane industries, draw France's production possibility frontier.*

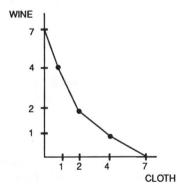

1.30 *Suppose that Germany is identical to the France of Problem 1.29. Draw the world production possibility frontier.*

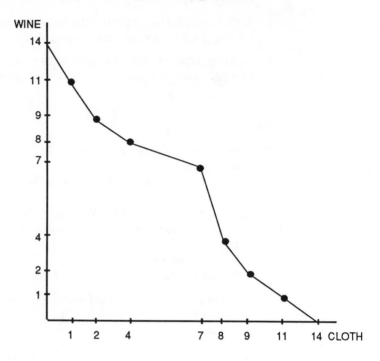

Additional Problems

1. What is the difference between increasing returns to scale and decreasing opportunity costs?

2. Give a practical example of increasing returns to scale that are internal to the firm, and a practical example of increasing returns to scale that are external to the firm.

Answers to Self-Test

1. 1.3.

2. 1.3.

11. Alternatives to Comparative Advantage: Product Differentiation and the Division of Labor

Basic Ideas

1. National economies of scale furnish a basis for trade, quite distinct from comparative advantage, in which the pattern of specialization is unimportant: what matters is that countries specialize in something.

2. This is not the case with international economies of scale, which could help reconcile comparative advantage to actual trade patterns.

3. International economies of scale due to a global division of labor and product differentiation in consumer goods imply that trade between countries with modest comparative cost differences will be largely intra-industry, and trade between countries with major comparative cost differences will be largely inter-industry.

4. Terms to know: **national economies of scale, international economies of scale, division of labor, product differentiation, monopolistic competition.**

Solution to Problem from the Text

1.32 *Suppose that scale economies are due to the division of labor, and that there are two countries. Discuss the relation between the production possibility frontiers of the two countries and the world.*

The shape of each country's production possibility frontier would depend upon actual production in the other country.

Additional Problem

Suppose that Table 1.10 in the text can be extended, with each additional unit of butane beyond the 7th requiring one additional unit of labor. Suppose also that the table applies to the butane industry, that the scale economies it depicts are *international*, and that in each country one unit of labor is required to produce each apple. France and Germany each have 10 units of labor.

a. Draw France's production possibility frontier if Germany produces only apples.

b. Draw France's production possibility frontier if Germany's labor force is divided equally between the two sectors.

c. Draw the world production possibility frontier.

d. Draw the world production possibility frontier if the scale economies in the butane industry are instead *national*.

12. Alternatives to Comparative Advantage: Oligopoly

Basic Ideas

1. If an industry is an oligopoly, international trade can increase the degree of competition, relative to autarky. This is a distinct reason to trade.

2. Oligopoly can generate two-way trade in identical commodities.

3. International trade is likely to lower oligopolistic profit and to benefit consumers.

4. Terms to know: **oligopoly, duopoly, reaction curve, quantity competition, price competition.**

Self-Test

1. Multiple choice: The intra-industry trade of differentiated goods may be explained by:
   1.1. Comparative advantage.
   1.2. Economies of scale.
   1.3. Oligopoly.
   1.4. All of the above.
   1.5. None of the above.

2. Multiple choice: The intra-industry trade of identical goods may be explained by:
   1.1. Comparative advantage.
   1.2. Economies of scale.
   1.3. Oligopoly.
   1.4. All of the above.
   1.5. None of the above.

Solution to Problem from the Text

1.33 *This section of the text made five basic points about trade and oligopoly when firms compete in quantities. Discuss in detail how valid each point remains if instead the firms compete in prices.*

You should be able to use Figure 1.14 in the text to duplicate fairly closely the reasoning that accompanied Figure 1.13.

Answers to Self-Test

1. 1.4.

2. 1.3.

13. Review Questions

1. Explain the principle of comparative advantage.

2. What is intra-industry trade and how prevalent is it? Give three alternative possible explanations for its existence. Do the alternatives have different welfare implications?

3. This chapter discussed three alternative reasons for trade. What do the three imply about policy regarding North-South trade?

4. Compare and contrast U.S.-Canadian trade with U.S.-Japanese trade.

CHAPTER 2   **Reciprocal Demand**

1. There's No Such Thing as a Free Lunch

Basic Ideas

1. A demand for a good, service, or asset is at the same time an offer to exchange something of equal value for it. Thus the total value of everything demanded by any individual must always equal the total value of everything supplied.

2. Since the above is true for every individual, it must also be true for collections of individuals, such as a country or group of countries.

3. This is *Walras's Law*: the aggregate value of all excess demands always equals zero.

4. If the only markets are for importables and exportables, Walras's Law says that the demand for imports is always equal in value to the supply of exports.

5. Terms to know: **equilibrium condition, identity, excess demand, excess supply.**

Self-Test

Next to each sentence write an I if what is described is analogous to an identity or an E if it is more like an equilibrium condition.

1. Price adjusts to equilibrate supply and demand.

2. Price is how much money you must pay for something.

3. A ball is a smooth spherical plaything.

4. An undisturbed ball will not begin to roll on a level surface.

Solutions to Problems from the Text

2.1 *Suppose that in addition to apples and butane there are 9,998 other markets in the French economy. Then what does an excess demand for apples imply? If the other 9,999 markets are in equilibrium, what must be true of the apple market?*

An excess demand for apples implies that the total value of the excess supply of machinery and the other 9,998 goods is positive. If the other 9,999 markets are in equilibrium, the apple market must be also.

2.2 Fill in the blanks in the following table.

Price of Apples in Terms of Butane	Excess Demand for Apples	Excess Demand for Butane
1/10	1000	
1/5		-80
1/2		-20
2/3	0	
1	-10	
3/2		30
2		50
5		100
10	-15	

Price of Apples in Terms of Butane	Excess Demand for Apples	Excess Demand for Butane
1/10	1000	-100
1/5	400	-80
1/2	40	-20
2/3	0	0
1	-10	10
3/2	-20	30
2	-25	50
5	-20	100
10	-15	150

2.3 *A man sold a bond for $10,000, bought a $7,000 automobile, and put the remaining $3,000 in the bank. Since the value of the bond supplied exceeded the value of the car demanded, did he not violate Walras's Law?*

Walras's Law is satisfied because the value of the bond supplied ($10,000) equals the sum of the values of the car demanded ($7,000) plus that of the bank deposit demanded ($3,000).

Additional Problem

Answer Problem 2.2 above if the first column is changed to "Price of Butane in Terms of Apples" and the second column to "Excess Supply of Apples."

1. *E.*

2. *I.*

3. *I.*

4. *E.*

2. Import Demand Curves

Basic Ideas

1. An import demand curve records how much a country would be willing to import at each hypothetical price of imports in terms of exports.

2. The volume of exports that a country would wish to trade at any particular point on its import demand curve is given by the product of imports times price at that point.

3. Because it merely summarizes what a single country would do under all conceivable circumstances, an import demand curve depends only upon information pertaining to that country, and it itself cannot indicate what international prices will be.

Self-Test

1. True or false: a country's import demand curve cannot tell us what relative prices are because the curve describes only the demand side of the economy and says nothing about the supply side.

2. True or false: a country's import demand curve cannot tell us what relative prices are because the curve describes only the supply side of the economy and says nothing about the demand side.

3. How is a country's import demand curve affected by each of the following:
   3.1. Domestic residents develop an increased dislike for foreign goods.
   3.2. Foreign residents develop an increased dislike for domestic goods.
   3.3. Foreign labor becomes more efficient.

Solutions to Problems from the Text

2.4 *Graph the observations in the completed table from Problem 2.2 and "connect the dots" to draw an import demand curve.*

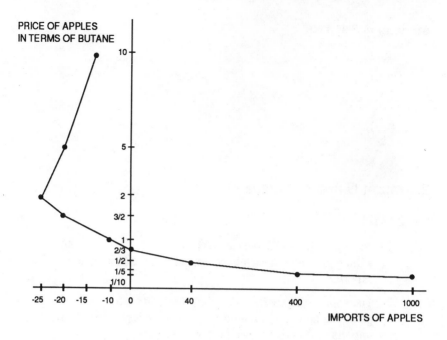

2.5 *Use the completed table from Problem 2.2 to graph an "export supply curve" showing the supply of exports of butane corresponding to each price of butane in terms of apples.*

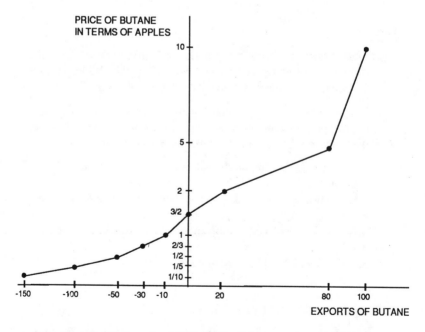

2.6 *Suppose France has 100 apples and no butane. The French tastes are such that the country would wish to behave as follows:*

If the Price of Butane in Terms of Apples is:	The French Wish to:
greater than 3 Apples	consume only Apples
3 Apples	export 60 Apples
not more than 2 Apples	consume 20 Apples

Use Walras's Law to deduce M^F and X^F for each case. Draw the French import demand curve by graphing the observations and connecting them. Also draw the French export supply curve.

See the statement of Problem 4.12 below.

2.7 *Suppose you have the following data for Germany:*

$$\frac{P_B}{P_A} = \frac{ExcD_A}{ExcD_B}$$

P_B/P_A	B demand	B supply	A demand	A supply
4		120	140	20
4/3	80	110		30
1	100	100	50	
2/3	140	80	45	85

Fill in the blanks. Draw Germany's import demand curve for apples by graphing the observations and connecting the dots. Also draw Germany's export supply curve.

See the statement of Problem 4.11 below.

*2.8 *Suppose that in England 5 units of labor are required to produce either a bolt of cloth or a cask of wine, that England has 100 units of labor, and that each Englishman always consumes one cask of wine for each bolt of cloth that he consumes. Derive England's import demand curve exactly.*

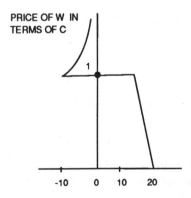

PRICE OF W IN TERMS OF C

*2.9 *Suppose that in Portugal 4 units of labor can produce a bolt of cloth, 1 labor unit can produce a cask of wine, 100 labor units are available, and each Portuguese always spends one-half of her*

-27-

income on each good. Derive Portugal's import demand curve exactly.

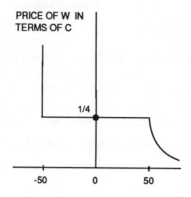

PRICE OF W IN
TERMS OF C

1/4

-50   0   50

Additional Problems

1. Trade in commodities can be regarded as indirect trade in the services of the primary factor embodied in the goods. Derive the exact shapes of the "factoral" import demand curves for the English and Portuguese economies described in Problems *2.8 and *2.9.

2. Using the data from Problem 2.7, draw Germany's export supply curve for butane, export supply curve for apples, and import demand curve for butane.

Answers to Self-Test

1. False.

2. False.

3. The effect on the import demand curve will be:
   3.1. It shifts toward the price axis, as domestic residents become less willing to import at each price.
   3.2. No effect.
   3.3. No effect.

*3. Exploring Further: Income and Substitution Effects

Basic Ideas

1. An improvement in the terms of trade—a reduction in the relative price of imports—influences a country in two basic ways.

2. Since imports are cheaper relative to exports, consumers substitute importables for exportables in their consumption patterns, and

producers substitute exportables for importables in their production patterns. Thus this substitution effect raises both imports and exports.

3. Since the country can now buy the same quantity of imports as before at a lower price, its income has in effect risen. This income effect will normally raise imports and lower exports.

4. Thus the income and substitution effects reinforce each other with respect to imports but work at cross purposes with regard to exports.

Solution to Problem from the Text

*2.10 *Discuss the roles of income and substitution effects in Problems *2.8 and *2.9.*

The flat parts of both curves reflect substitution in production. When the countries specialize in the production of exportables, there are no longer any production substitution effects, and in the case of England there are no consumption substitution effects because, by assumption, the residents of this country are unwilling to substitute one good for the other. Thus the backward-bending part of England's curve reflects pure income effects. The vertical and downward sloping parts of the Portuguese import demand curve, on the other hand, illustrate an income effect exactly neutralized by a consumption substitution effect with regard to exports.

Additional Problems

1. Discuss the significance of income and substitution effects in the response of oil importers to the oil price rises of the 1970s, and with respect to the oil price declines of the 1980s.

2. Discuss the influence of income and substitution effects on the shape of the import demand curve if exports are inferior. If imports are inferior. (An *inferior* good is one that we consume less of as our income rises, like gruel and secondhand clothes.)

4. The Volume and Terms of Trade

Basic Ideas

1. International equilibrium is described by the intersection of one country's import demand curve with the other country's export supply curve, because only there is the amount one country wants to import just equal to what the other wants to export while at the same time what the former wants to export is what the latter wants to import.

2. The two curves must be drawn consistently. That is, if positive movements on an axis measure off imports for one country they must measure exports for the other, etc.

Solutions to Problems from the Text

2.11 *Draw Figure 2.3 in the textbook as it would look if France had the comparative advantage in butane.*

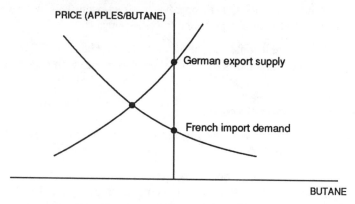

PRICE (APPLES/BUTANE)

German export supply

French import demand

BUTANE

Suppose that France and Germany, as described in Problems 2.6 and 2.7, enter into free trade. By drawing the French import demand and German export supply curves find the terms of trade and volume of goods exchanged. Do the same with French export supply and German import demand curves.

France exports 70 apples to Germany for 30 butane, so that

$P_B/P_A = 7/3$.

*2.13 *Suppose that the England and Portugal described in Problems *2.8 and *2.9 engage in free trade. What will the terms of trade between these countries be? Who exports how much of what? What are the wages and prices in the two countries? Now suppose that England's labor force increases to 1,000 units and nothing else changes. Which curves shift? What are the new terms of trade and pattern of trade? What size must England's labor force be if that country is to export wine?*

England specializes in cloth production and exports 4 to Portugal in exchange for 16 casks of wine. If England's wage = 1, $P_C = 5$ and Portugal's wage is 5/4, so that $P_W = 5/4$. (These prices and wages can be any common multiple of these numbers, so long as they maintain the same relation to each other.) If England's labor force increases to 1,000, its import demand curve shifts out from the origin by a factor of ten, and Portugal's import demand curve is unaffected. In the new equilibrium, England now produces both goods, exporting 50 cloth to Portugal for 50 wine. England would never export wine, since it has a comparative advantage in cloth.

Additional Problem

Draw Figure 2.3 of the text as it would appear if neither country had a comparative advantage in anything, that is, if autarky prices in the two countries were equal.

5. Elasticity

Basic Ideas

1. The shape of an import demand curve at a point can be described by its import elasticity: the percentage increase in imports caused by a one percent improvement in the terms of trade.

2. The shape can alternatively be described by the export elasticity and by the elasticity of exports with respect to imports. Since they describe the same thing in different ways, these elasticities are all related to each other.

3. Things to know: **how to measure e geometrically;**

   $f = e - 1;\ g = f/e.$

Self-Test

1. Micronia is so small that nothing it could conceivably do would influence world prices. What can you say about the elasticity of the rest of the world's import demand curve?

2. Petrolia produces one billion barrels of oil each and every year but has no use for the stuff. The country accordingly exports the oil for whatever it will fetch on world markets. What can you say about the elasticity of Petrolia's export supply curve?

Solutions to Problems from the Text

2.14 *Suppose you have the following observations:*

p	M	X
100		100,000
99	1,030	

Fill in the blanks. Calculate e, f, and g for the change from the first observation to the second.

p	M	X
100	1,000	100,000
99	1,030	101,970

$e = (100/1000)\ (30/1) = 3;$

$f = (100/100{,}000)\ (1970/1) = 1.97 \approx 2 = e - 1;$

$g = (1000/100{,}000)(1970/30) = .66 \approx 2/3 \approx f/e.$

2.15 *In Problem 2.2 calculate* e, f, *and* g *for each pair of successive observations, using the definition of each elasticity. Also calculate* f *and* g *from your values of* e *using the relationships derived above. Try to explain any discrepancies.*

From the definitions, when the price of apples in terms of butane falls from 1/5 to 1/10:

$e = [(1000 - 400)/400]/[\{(1/5) - (1/10)\}/\{1/5\}] = [3/2]/[1/2] = 3;$

$f = [(100 - 80)/80]/[1/2] = [1/4]/[1/2] = 1/2;$

$g = [1/4]/[3/2] = 1/6.$

The formula $e = f - 1$ is an approximation that becomes more accurate for smaller changes in prices.

*2.16 *What can you say about the elasticities of the curves you derived in Problems *2.8 and *2.9?*

On those parts of the English and Portuguese import demand curves that are horizontal, e and f are infinite and g is unity. On the other parts of the Portuguese import demand curve, $f = g = 0$ and $e = 1$. On the other parts of the English import demand curve

$f < 0, g < 0,$ and $e < 1.$

Additional Problems

1. In view of the description of trade between the DCs and the LDCs given in Chapter 1 of the textbook, speculate about the elasticities of the import demand curves of these country groups.

2. Draw Figure 2.3 in the textbook as it would look if there were several alternative international equilibria, rather than just one. What seems to be the role of elasticities?

Answers to Self-Test

1. e and f are infinite, and g is unity.

2. $f = 0,$ and so $e = 1$ and $g = 0.$

6. Some International Economic Problems of the Less Developed Countries

Basic Ideas

1. Trade between the DCs and the LDCs seems to be characterized by low elasticities, and these are relevant to several issues involving that trade which are the subject of much concern and debate.

2. These are: fluctuations in LDC export earnings; potential control over

the terms of trade; an alleged secular deterioration in the LDCs' terms of trade.

3. Attempts to come to grips with these issues on a multilateral basis have suffered from the "free rider" problem with regard to LDCs and from a divergence of national interests between DCs and LDCs.

4. Be sure that you understand: **the nature of the free rider problem; the specific demands comprising the proposal for a "New International Economic Order."**

Solutions to Problems from the Text

2.18 *The alleged secular decline in the LDCs' terms of trade was explained by low elasticities and the relative shifts of import demand and export supply curves. How would the argument be affected by elastic curves? What is the role of elasticity.*

The argument is qualitatively the same when elasticities are high, but it would not be as serious because the relative shifts of the import demand curves would cause more modest price changes.

2.19 *Unilateral action is unlikely to be effective, because an individual LDC faces a much more elastic import demand curve than do LDCs in the aggregate. But if so, how could the three issues ever arise for individual countries?*

They arise for individual countries because they arise for the entire aggregate.

2.22 *Suppose that the LDCs succeed in improving their terms of trade by interfering with free trade in world markets. This makes the DCs worse off. Suppose the latter are considering using foreign aid as a bribe to induce the LDCs to return to free trade. Is it possible for the DCs to offer a tempting bribe, that is, one large enough so that the LDCs are at least as well off as they are now but not so large that the DCs are worse off? Why?*

Yes. Free trade is efficient for the world as a whole, so that a movement to it will benefit the DCs by more than it harms the LDCs. This means that the former can afford to fully compensate the latter and still be better off themselves.

7. "Elasticity Optimism" and "Elasticity Pessimism": Empirical Estimates

Basic Ideas

1. The basic idea behind reciprocal demand is that the international economy works through relative price adjustments.

2. Elasticity is basically a measure of how effective relative price changes are. Accordingly, it is not surprising that low elasticities are associated with problems.

3. "Elasticity optimists" believe that price elasticities are high and "elasticity pessimists" believe that they are low.

4. Manufactures tend to be more price elastic than primary products. Thus trade among the DCs, which involves a lot of intra-industry exchange of manufactures, seems to be characterized by relatively high elasticities, and DC-LDC trade, where manufactures are typically exchanged for primary products, seems to feature lower elasticities.

5. A "small" country is one that cannot influence the international prices at which it trades. It thus faces an infinitely elastic (import demand or export supply) curve from the rest of the world.

Self-Test

1. True or false: A small country has an infinitely elastic import demand curve.

2. What is the "identification problem"?

Solutions to Problems from the Text

2.23 *Suppose we represent a restrictive national trade policy by a shift in a country's import demand curve that causes it to demand fewer imports at each price, or by a shift of its export supply curve that causes it to supply fewer exports at each price. Discuss the effects of such a policy shift by each of the countries depicted in Figure 2.7 of the textbook.*

a. Such a shift by Luxembourg reduces the volume of trade but has no effect on price.

b. Such a shift by the importer reduces both the volume of trade and the price; if done by an exporter it also reduces the volume of trade but raises the price.

c. Same as in b, except that the volume effects are relatively smaller and the price effects relatively larger.

2.24 *When is a shift in a country's import demand curve that causes it to demand fewer imports at each price the same as a shift of its export supply curve that causes it to supply fewer exports at each price?*

Always.

Answers to Self-Test

1. False.

2. The problem of fitting data points to estimate a curve when it is not known whether the data reflect movements along the curve or shifts of the curve.

*8. Exploring Further: How to Derive Import Demand and Export Supply Curves

Basic Ideas

1. This section shows how to derive geometrically a country's import demand curve from its production possibility frontier and a set of community indifference curves.

2. The technique allows you to see the relation between a country's import demand and export supply curves, and how each relates to the *offer curve*: a third method of recording exactly the same information.

3. Be sure you understand: **offer curve**.

Solutions to Problems from the Text

2.25 *In Figure 2.10 of the textbook, derive a French export supply curve of butane and import demand curve for apples.*

The respective answers are the same as panels (a) and (b) of Figure 2.11 in the text, except that the horizontal axis is measured in the opposite direction, i.e., each curve should be "flipped over" the vertical axis.

2.26 *What would the offer curve in Figure 2.11 of the textbook look like if exports were measured on the butane axis and imports on the apple axis?*

The curve would have the opposite curvature. If an offer curve is imagined to be a bowl, it will "hold" its import axes; thus in this problem the curve should bend so that it "holds" the positive part of the apple axis and the negative part of the butane axis.

2.27 *Suppose that in England 5 units of labor are required to produce either a bolt of cloth or a cask of wine, that England has 100 units of labor, and that each English resident always consumes one cask of wine for each bolt of cloth. Use the techniques of this section to derive England's import demand, export supply, and offer curves.*

The English offer curve:

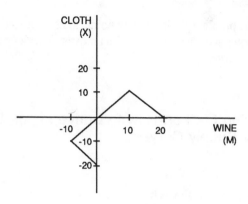

Additional Problems

1. Using indifference curves, production possibility frontiers, and import demand curves, show that:
   1.1. Free trade is always better for a country than autarky;
   1.2. Free trade is efficient in the sense that it is impossible to make one country better off without harming the other; and
   1.3. Limited trade may be better or worse than free trade for a single country.

2. Show geometrically that the income effect is very small near the origin on the import demand curve.

3. Use the techniques of this section to derive the import demand curve of Portugal, as described in Problem *2.9 in the text.

*9. Exploring Further: Stability of International Equilibrium

Basic Ideas

1. An equilibrium is *stable* if an economy will automatically go there if it starts off somewhere else.

2. Stability depends upon how an economy behaves when not in equilibrium, so some "disequilibrium hypothesis" is necessary before stability can be investigated.

3. A common hypothesis is that price will be rising in a market experiencing excess demand. If this hypothesis is accurate, an equilibrium will be stable if the import demand curves at that equilibrium satisfy the *Marshall-Lerner condition*.

4. Terms to know: **stability; disequilibrium hypothesis; multiple equilibria; Marshall-Lerner condition.**

Solutions to Problems from the Text

2.28 *Express the Marshall-Lerner condition in terms of the f's; the g's.*

$f^F + f^G > -1; g^F g^G < 1.$

2.29 *What can you say about the stability of an equilibrium in which one of the countries has the import demand curve you derived in Problem *2.8.*

If the equilibrium occurs on the part of England's import demand curve that is horizontal, that equilibrium must be stable, since England's import demand curve has an import elasticity equal to infinity there. But along the parts of the import demand curve that bend back, England's import elasticity is at most 1/2, so equilibrium cannot possibly be stable if the foreign import demand curve's elasticity is no greater than 1/2.

2.30 *Suppose the disequilibrium hypothesis of this section is not true and that an equilibrium can be stable even if the Marshall-Lerner condition fails. Draw Figures 2.5 and 2.9 in the textbook with the condition violated. How does this effect the discussion of policy issues in sections 6, 7, and 9 of the text?*

In this case a shift of an import demand curve produces the opposite effect on the terms of trade from that shown in the textbook, with a resultant reversal of policy issues.

2.31 *Suppose that England has the import demand curve of Problem *2.8 but that in Problem *2.9 each Portuguese instead always consumes one cask of wine with each two bolts of cloth. Derive Portugal's export supply curve. For what sizes of the Portuguese and British labor forces does an unstable equilibrium exist?*

Never.

Additional Problems

1. What can you say about the stability of an equilibrium in which one of the countries has the import demand curve you derived in Problem *2.9.?

2. Derive the Marshall-Lerner condition algebraically. Use the calculus to formulate a precise definition of e and to derive the condition. Check your answer by reading section A.3 of Appendix I of the textbook.

10. Review Questions

1. Explain the basic idea of reciprocal demand.

2. Write an essay on the concept of *elasticity* of import demand. Be sure you discuss: what it is, why it matters, empirical evidence.

3. Discuss international economic problems facing the LDCs.

4. Many of the international economic issues confronting the LDCs are also of concern to the DCs. For some of these the interests of the two blocs coincide, and for others they are in conflict. Give examples of each and discuss the importance of this consideration for policy measures.

5. Research attempts to establish and maintain international coffee agreements. Describe the details of actual agreements and their histories. Interpret in terms of the theory presented in this chapter.

CHAPTER 3   The Basis of Comparative Advantage

1. The Heckscher-Ohlin-Samuelson Model

Basic Ideas

1. The Heckscher-Ohlin theory postulates that differences in relative factor endowments between countries is the cause of the pattern of comparative advantage.

2. The principal theoretical tool used to expound, investigate, and apply this hypothesis is the Heckscher-Ohlin-Samuelson model.

3. This abstract structure assumes: two countries, goods and factors; the two countries are identical in every respect except factor endowments; factors are immobile between countries but mobile between industries within a country; technology is characterized by constant returns to scale and is available to the two countries equally.

4. Be sure you know: **constant returns to scale, factor abundance, factor intensity.**

Self-Test

1. Which of the following is inconsistent with the Heckscher-Ohlin-Samuelson model:
   1.1. The home country trades with three others.
   1.2. Technology has increasing returns to scale.
   1.3. America has more land per worker than Europe, but about the same amount of capital per worker.
   1.4 Increasing opportunity cost.
   1.5. England exports cloth and machines and imports wine.
   1.6. Italians are more fond of wine than the residents of the rest of the world.

2. Suppose that there is only one known combination of capital and labor that can produce a unit of butane, but there are many ways to produce apples (that is, the two factors can easily be substituted for each other). What does this imply about the relative capital intensity of the two industries?

Solutions to Problems from the Text

3.1 *Recall the discussion of U.S. trade patterns in section 11 of chapter 1 of the textbook. Try to explain the apparent U.S. comparative advantage in terms of relative factor endowments (do not confine yourself to capital and labor; try to think of other relevant factors).*

U.S. exports could suggest an abundance of highly skilled labor and temperate-zone agricultural land. Imports could suggest a relative scarcity of other labor and mineral-laden land.

3.2 *Suppose that England has 100 workers and 160 units of capital, whereas Portugal has 100 workers and 70 units of capital. Also suppose that each cask of wine requires 4 workers and 1 unit of capital to produce, whereas each bolt of cloth requires 5 units of capital and 2 workers. Apply the definitions of factor abundance and factor intensity.*

Since $160/100 > 70/100$, England is capital abundant relative to Portugal; since $5/2 > 1/4$, cloth is capital intensive relative to wine.

Additional Problem

In view of what you have learned about trade between the DCs and the LDCs, speculate about the relative factor abundance of these two groups of countries. About the relative factor intensities of their export industries.

Answers to Self-Test

1. All except 1.4.

2. The relative capital intensity of the two industries would depend upon which technique was actually in use in the apple industry, and that would presumably depend upon the cost of capital and labor.

2. A Basic Relationship

Basic Ideas

1. An increase in wages relative to rents raises the cost of producing the labor-intensive good relative to the cost of producing the capital-intensive good.

2. The relation between relative factor prices and relative commodity

costs is a technological one and so is identical for both countries, in the context of the Heckscher-Ohlin-Samuelson model.

3. The cost of a commodity must equal its price if that good is actually produced, in equilibrium, but might exceed price in a country that does not produce the good.

Self-Test

1. How is the relation between wages relative to rents and the cost of the labor-intensive good relative to that of the capital-intensive good affected by each of the following:
   1.1. An increase in population.
   1.2. A movement from free trade to autarky.
   1.3. An increase in wages relative to rents.
   1.4. A uniform increase in labor efficiency.
   1.5. An increased demand for the capital-intensive good.

2. In Figure 3.1 of the textbook, suppose that the price of butane in terms of apples is equal to the distance *OB*. What must be true if the wage rental ratio is less than the distance *OA*? If greater than *OA*?

Solutions to Problems from the Text

3.4 Draw Figure 3.1 in the textbook as it would appear if butane production were capital intensive. What would the curve look like if, by a fluke of nature, butane and apples used exactly the same technique of production?

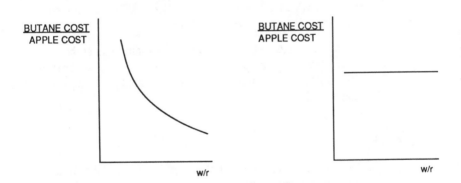

3.5 *Derive a curve, like that in Figure 3.1 in the textbook, for England, where each cask of wine requires 4 workers and 1 unit of capital to produce and each bolt of cloth requires 2 workers and 5 units of capital. What could you conclude about English production if the wage and the rent in England both equaled 1 and the price of cloth in terms of wine was 2?*

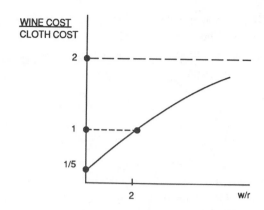

$$\frac{\text{(wine cost)}}{\text{(cloth cost)}} = \frac{(4w + r)}{(2w + 5r)} = \frac{4(w/r) + 1}{2(w/r) + 5}$$

If $w = r = 1$, then (wine cost)/(cloth cost) = 5/7 > 1/2, so England would produce only cloth.

3.6 *Suppose that, as a result of some innovation, it is now possible to produce butane with fewer workers per unit of capital than before. No change occurs in the apple technology. What is the effect on the curve in Figure 3.1 of the textbook?*

It becomes flatter.

*3.7 *What would the curve in Figure 3.1 in the textbook look like if butane were relatively capital intensive at low wage-rental ratios but relatively labor intensive at high wage-rental ratios, with apples and butane using exactly the same technique at some intermediate wage-rental ratio? What circumstances could cause two industries to have this relation?*

The curve would be U-shaped, reaching a minimum at the intermediate wage rental ratio. This could happen if it were much easier to substitute capital for labor in the apple industry than in the butane industry.

Additional Problem

Each poobah requires 1 unit of land and 1 unit of labor in its production, whereas a zingo requires a total of 3 units of land and labor in any combination (including fractions). Draw the curve relating the relative cost of poobahs and zingoes to the relative prices of land and labor.

Answers to Self-Test

1. 1.1. No effect.
   1.2. No effect.
   1.3. No effect: a movement along the curve.

1.4. It would shift the curve down.

1.5. No effect.

2. If less than *OA* the country must be producing only butane, if greater than *OA* only apples.

3. The Heckscher-Ohlin Theory: Comparative Advantage and Factor Prices

Basic Ideas

1. This section discusses two of the four basic propositions developed in the Heckscher-Ohlin-Samuelson model.

2. The *Heckscher-Ohlin theorem* states that a country has a comparative advantage in the good making relatively intensive use of the country's relatively abundant factor.

3. The *factor-price equalization theorem* states that free trade will make the prices of each factor more nearly equal across countries, with complete equality taking place if both countries produce both goods.

4. These propositions share the property that each is demonstrated using the technological relation between relative costs and relative factor prices.

5. Things to know: **how to demonstrate each proposition geometrically.**

Self-Test

1. Which of the following observations is inconsistent with the others:
   1.1. France and Germany engage in free trade.
   1.2. France is relatively capital abundant.
   1.3. French firms employ more capital-intensive techniques than their German counterparts.
   1.4. Both countries produce both goods.
   1.5. It's raining everywhere.

2. True or false: free trade causes wages to equal rents if both countries produce both goods.

3. True or false: labor abundant countries export labor-intensive goods instead of labor.

Solutions to Problems from the Text

3.9 *Agricultural trade between the United States and Europe is not free. The yield per acre on a French farm is typically much higher than on an American farm devoted to the same crop. Does this indicate relative American inefficiency or backwardness? Explain in terms of the theory. What would you expect to be true of relative French and American prices of the relevant factors? What do you think would be the effect of a movement to free trade?*

France is obtaining higher yields per acre by using more capital and labor per acre than America; this indicates a relative abundance of land in America. Free trade would tend to equalize factor prices and so cause the two countries to utilize more similar techniques.

3.10 *Suppose that when each cask of wine produced requires 4 labor units and 1 capital unit in its production and each bolt of cloth requires 2 and 5 units respectively of labor and capital, the wage and the rent each equal 100. What is the cost of wine and cloth? Suppose the wage and rent both increase to 110. By what percentage have they risen? What are the new costs of the two goods and by what percentages have they changed? Answer the same questions if instead the wage increases from 100 to 120 and the rent from 100 to 105. Answer the questions if instead the wage falls from 100 to 90 while the rent rises from 100 to 120.*

Wine cost = 4 x 100 + 1 x 100 = 500 and cloth cost = 2 x 100 + 5 x 100 = 700. Both w and r rise by 10 percent. Now: wine cost = 4 x 110 + 1 x 110 = 550 and cloth cost = 2 x 110 + 5 x 110 = 770. Thus the cost of wine has increased by 10 percent, as has the cost of cloth. If instead the wage increases to 120 and the rent to 105, wine cost goes up to 585 and cloth cost to 765; thus the percentage increases are: 20 percent (wages) > 17 percent (wine) > 9.3 percent (cloth) > 5 percent (capital). If the wage falls to 90 and the rent rises to 120, wine cost falls to 480 and cloth cost rises to 780. Thus the percentage increases are: 20 percent (wage) > 11.4 percent (cloth) > –4 percent (wine) > –10 percent (rent).

*3.11 *Discuss in detail the Heckscher-Ohlin and the factor-price equalization theorems in the context of Problem *3.7.*

Both propositions can be violated in such a case. This is illustrated below. Germany is labor abundant, and autarky relative factor prices in the two countries are indicated at F and G respectively. Note that Germany has a comparative advantage in apples, even though apples are capital intensive in Germany. (However France has a comparative advantage in butane which is capital intensive in France, the capital abundant country.) The free-trade relative price is indicated by p, with both countries producing both goods at factor prices indicated by F' and G' respectively. Not only has free trade failed to completely equalize factor prices, it has actually made them more unequal.

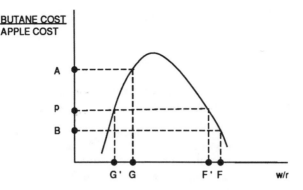

*3.12 *Suppose that we retain all of the assumptions of the Heckscher-Ohlin-Samuelson model, except that we assume that all French citizens have a much greater relative preference for apple consumption than all German citizens (who therefore have a much greater relative preference for butane consumption). How is the Heckscher-Ohlin theorem affected?*

No effect.

Additional Problems

1. Suppose that England and Portugal share the technology described in Problem 3.10 above, and that the other assumptions of the Heckscher-Ohlin-Samuelson model are satisfied. Suppose that in autarky the wage and rent each equal 100 in England while in Portugal the wage is 90 and the rent is 120. What does this indicate about the relative factor abundance of the two countries? Show that the Heckscher-Ohlin theorem is demonstrated.

2. Suppose that Portugal and England, as described in the preceding problem, enter into free trade. The international price of wine is 550 and that of cloth is 770. Both countries continue to produce both goods. Show how the factor-price equalization theorem is demonstrated.

3. How is the factor-price equalization theorem affected in the context of Problem *3.12 above?

Answers to Self-Test

1. 1.3.

2. False.

3. True.

4. The Heckscher-Ohlin Theory: Income Distribution and Growth

Basic Ideas

1. This section discusses the remaining two of the four basic propositions derived from the Heckscher-Ohlin-Samuelson model.

2. The *Stolper-Samuelson theorem* says that an increase in the relative price of a good will cause the price of the factor used intensively in the production of that good to rise relative to both commodities and the price of the other factor to fall relative to both commodities.

3. The *Rybczynski theorem* says that an increase in the relative endowment of a factor, at constant prices, increases the output of the good making intensive use of that factor relative to both factor endowments, and reduces the output of the other good relative to both endowments.

4. The two theorems are proved by a very similar logic.

5. Points to know: **how to prove the two theorems; how they relate to income distribution and growth; real income; how to spell "Rybczynski."**

Self-Test

1. The Heckscher-Ohlin-Samuelson model makes several strong assumptions. Which of the following is not required for either the Stolper-Samuelson or the Rybczynski theorem to be valid:
    1.1. The two countries share the same technology.
    1.2. There are two goods and two factors.
    1.3. Tastes are identical in the two countries.
    1.4. Within each country the two factors are freely mobile between the two industries.

2. Multiple choice: If the price of apples rises by 10 percent and the price of butane falls by 10 percent, while factor prices do not change, Crazy Harry's real income:
    2.1. Rises.
    2.2. Falls.
    2.3. Is unchanged because the average price change is 0 percent.
    2.4. Rises if and only if Crazy Harry spends more than half his income on butane.

Solutions to Problems from the Text

3.13 *What do you think is the consequence of the historic rise in the American wage, relative to other factor prices, on the cost of a university education? On the cleanliness of city streets? Specifically relate your answers to the theory.*

Since both activities are relatively labor-intensive, their prices should have increased more rapidly than prices generally.

3.14 *Show how your answers to Problem 3.10 illustrate the Stolper-Samuelson theorem.*

When the cost of labor-intensive apples rose relative to that of capital-intensive cloth, the wage rose proportionally more than both and the rent proportionally less than both.

3.15 *The savings rate in Japan since the Second World War has been much higher than in most other countries. What is the likely effect on relative Japanese factor abundance? Use the theory of this section to predict the likely consequences.*

The high savings rate should allow much capital accumulation, causing Japan to become relatively more capital abundant compared to the rest of the world. This would likely cause an even more rapid rise in the production of capital intensive goods, and therefore lead to increases in their exports of these goods.

3.16 *Suppose that the country described in Problem 3.10 above produces 200 casks of wine and 200 bolts of cloth. How much capital and labor is this economy using? Suppose wine output falls to 80 casks. What are the changes in percentage terms? How much capital and labor is now required? What are these changes in percentage terms? How does this illustrate the Rybczynski theorem?*

The 200 casks of wine require 800 labor and 200 capital whereas the 200 cloth require 400 labor and 1,000 capital, for a total of 1,200 labor and 1,200 capital. If the output of wine falls to 80, 480 less labor and 120 less capital will be required. Thus wine output falls 60 percent, labor usage falls 40 percent, capital usage 10 percent, and cloth output 0 percent.

3.17 *Calculate the outputs of wine and cloth in Portugal and England if the countries have the technology described in Problem 3.10 above, if England has 100 workers and 160 capital units, and if Portugal has 100 workers and 70 capital units. (Do this either by trial and error or by setting up and solving two simultaneous equations in two unknowns.) Show how a comparison of Portugal and England illustrates the Rybczynski theorem. Show how it also demonstrates the Heckscher-Ohlin theorem, if the two countries are freely trading.*

In England: $W + 5C = 160$ (capital) and $4W + 2C = 100$ (labor). These have the solution $W = 10$ and $C = 30$.

In Portugal: $W + 5C = 70$ (capital) and $4W + 2C = 100$ (labor). These have the solution $W = 20$ and $C = 10$.

Thus:

$$\left(\frac{30 - 10}{10} = 3\right) > \left(\frac{160 - 70}{70} = \frac{9}{7}\right) >$$

$$\left(\frac{100 - 100}{100} = 0\right) > \left(\frac{10 - 20}{10} = -1\right)$$

which illustrates the Rybczynski theorem.

*3.19 *The Stolper-Samuelson and Rybczynski theorems apply to situations in which both goods are actually produced. Suppose instead that France specializes completely in the production of apples. How would French wages and rents be affected by a rise in the price of apples? By a rise in the price of butane? How are real wages affected? How would French outputs respond to a change in factor endowments, with the prices of apples and butane unchanged?*

A rise in the price of apples would raise both wages and rents in the same proportion, thereby increasing the real wage of anyone who spent any part of her income on butane and holding constant the real wage of any person consuming only apples. A rise in the price of butane would leave wages and rents unchanged, thereby lowering the real wage of anyone who spent any part of his income on butane and holding constant the real wage of any person consuming only apples. An increase in either factor endowment would increase the output of apples.

*3.20 *The Stolper-Samuelson theorem assumes that both factors are freely mobile between industries within a country. But in fact this is not true, at least for substantial time periods. Suppose, for example, that labor is freely mobile between apple and butane production but that capital is immobile, so that each industry's capital stock is fixed. Discuss the Stolper-Samuelson theorem in this case.*

For the answer to this problem, read section 11 of chapter 3 of the textbook.

Additional Problems

1. Suppose that we depart from the Heckscher-Ohlin-Samuelson model by allowing three factors of production (land, labor, and capital), rather than just two, all of which are used in the production of each of the two goods. Suppose that both goods are in fact being produced, and that one of them rises in price. Go through the proof of the Stolper-Samuelson theorem in the textbook, noting exactly how the argument is changed or not.

2. Suppose that we depart from the Heckscher-Ohlin-Samuelson model by allowing three goods (apples, butane, and cloth), rather than just

two, each of which uses both factors. Suppose that the endowment of one of these factors increases, all prices remaining unchanged. Go through the proof of the Rybczynski theorem in the textbook, noting exactly how the argument is changed or not.

Answers to Self-Test

1. 1.1 and 1.3.

2. 2.4.

*5. Exploring Further: Analysis of the Heckscher-Ohlin-Samuelson Model—the Firm

Basic Ideas

1. This section gives a geometric treatment of the behavior of a competitive firm.

2. Such a firm will minimize its costs if it chooses the technique of production where the marginal rate of technical substitution equals (minus) the ratio of the respective factor prices.

3. Things to know: **isoquant, constant returns to scale, marginal rate of technical substitution**.

Solutions to Problems from the Text

3.21 *Suppose that the production of each bushel of apples requires 4 (or more) units of capital together with 2 (or more) units of labor. Draw the one-bushel isoquant.*

What can you say about the MRTS$_{KL}^{A}$ in this case?

What techniques of production would an apple producer choose if w/r = 5? If w/r = 1? For other values of w/r?

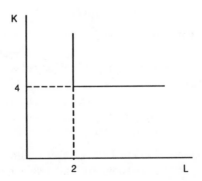

The technique $K = 4, L = 2$ would be chosen in all cases (where both w and r are positive).

3.22 *Suppose that each bolt of cloth requires 1 unit (or more) of capital plus 4 units (or more) of labor to produce. Answer the same questions as in Problem 3.21 above.*

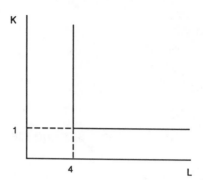

3.23 *Suppose that cloth can be produced either as described in Problem 3.22 or by using 7 (or more) units of capital plus 1 (or more) units of labor. Answer the same questions as in Problem 3.21 above.*

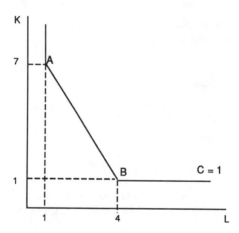

To the right of point B, the $MRTS_{KL}^{A}$ equals 0, above point A it is infinite, between the two points it equals 2, and at the points itself it is undefined. If $w/r = 5$, technique A would be used; if $w/r = 1$, B would be used; if $w/r = 2$, any technique between A and B inclusive could be used.

Additional Problems

1. Redraw Figure 3.8 in the textbook as it would look with both a butane isoquant and an apple isoquant drawn in the proper relation to each other when apples are relatively capital intensive.

2. Suppose that K units of capital and L units of labor can always produce $(KL)^{1/2}$ bushels of apples. Answer the questions of Problem 3.21 above.

*6. Exploring Further: Analysis of the Heckscher-Ohlin-Samuelson Model—the General Equilibrium of Production

Basic Ideas

1. This section presents a geometric method for finding the factor prices and production pattern in an economy, given commodity prices and endowments.

2. Thing to know: **how to use Figure 3.9 in the textbook.**

Self-Test

1. Suppose that the technology for producing apples is identical to that for producing butane. Draw a diagram like that of Figure 3.9 in the textbook for each of the following cases. Using your diagrams, say what will be produced in each case.
   1.1. The price of apples exceeds that of butane.
   1.2. The price of butane exceeds that of apples.
   1.3. The prices of apples and butane are equal.

Solutions to Problems from the Text

3.25 *Suppose each wine cask requires 4 units of capital and 2 of labor while each bolt of cloth requires 1 unit of capital and 4 of labor. What will be produced if the economy has 10 units of labor and 6 of capital? What will factor prices be if the price of wine is fr2 and that of cloth is fr1?*

   $4W + C = 6$ (capital) and $2W + 4C = 10$ (labor) have the solution $W = 1$ and $C = 2$.

   $4r + 2w = 2$ (price of wine) and $r + 4w = 1$ (price of cloth) have the solution $r = 3/7$ and $w = 1/7$.

3.26 *What will happen to the outputs of the two goods if, in Problem 3.25, the capital stock increases to 8 units? What happens to factor prices if the price of cloth increases to fr2?*

   W increases to $11/7$ and C falls to $12/7$; w increases to $3/7$ and r falls to $2/7$.

3.27 *The discussion in the textbook assumed that the economy-wide capital-labor ratio was between the least-cost capital-labor ratios in the two sectors, that is, that G in Figure 3.9 in the textbook was between the rays OQ and OR. What would happen if instead the economy's endowment were as indicated in Figure 3.9 by point H? By J?*

If the endowment point were H, the economy would specialize in apples and relative factor prices would be given by the slope of the apples isoquant passing through H. If the endowment point were J, the economy would specialize in butane and relative factor prices would be given by the slope of the butane isoquant passing through J.

*3.28 *How do your answers to Problem 3.25 change if a bolt of cloth can be produced* either *by the technique described in that problem, or by 7 units of capital plus 1 of labor?*

No change, because the original technique would still be the cheapest way to produce cloth.

*3.29 *Use isoquants to illustrate, in a diagram like Figure 3.9 in the textbook, the situation described in Problem *3.7 above.*

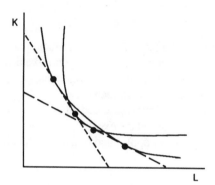

Additional Problems

1. How would the general equilibrium depicted in Figure 3.9 in the textbook be altered if P_A were to double?

2. How would the general equilibrium depicted in Figure 3.9 in the textbook be altered if the capital stock K were to double?

3. Suppose that an economy is producing both goods, as in Figure 3.9 in the textbook. Now introduce a third good, cloth, with its own distinctive isoquants. If the prices of apples and butane do not change, under what circumstances will cloth actually be produced instead of one of the other goods? When will all three goods be produced? Complete the parallelogram in this latter case.

Answer to Self-Test

1. The economy will
    1.1. Specialize in apple production.

1.2. Specialize in butane production.

1.3. Produce an indeterminate combination of apples and butane.

*7. Exploring Further: Analysis of the Heckscher-Ohlin-Samuelson Model—Basic Propositions

Basic Ideas

1. This section uses the geometry developed in the two preceding sections to demonstrate explicitly the four basic propositions of the Heckscher-Ohlin theory.

2. You should, of course, understand and be able to repeat the proofs of the propositions. Test your understanding by constructing numerical examples.

Additional Problems

1. Using the technology described in Problems 3.21 and 3.22, illustrate the four propositions with specific numerical examples.

2. In Figure 3.11 in the textbook, complete the parallelograms from point G to find the allocations of capital and labor to the industries both before and after the price change. Compare the two situations.

3. With your answer to Problem *3.29 as a starting point, draw a situation where two countries produce both goods while freely trading with each other, but nevertheless have unequal factor prices.

4. Because of identical tastes, two countries freely trading together will consume the two goods in identical proportions. If factor prices are equalized, the same production techniques will be used in the two countries, so they will "consume" factors in the same proportions (*i.e.*, the factors used to produce the goods they actually consume). Using the geometry developed in this and the preceding sections, depict the pattern of factor trade (in this indirect sense of the factors used to produce the goods actually traded) between two countries who continue to produce both goods.

8. The Specific-Factors Model

Basic Ideas

1. The Heckscher-Ohlin-Samuelson model assumes that both factors are freely mobile between industries within a single country. But limits to internal mobility are often important in practice.

2. The *specific-factors model* is a variant of the Heckscher-Ohlin-Samuelson model in which only one of the factors is mobile between industries. The other factor is specific to the industry in which it is located (that is, it cannot move between industries), but it is mobile between firms within that industry.

3. Factors are more likely to be mobile the more time they have to move. Thus the Heckscher-Ohlin-Samuelson model can be regarded as a long-run version of the specific-factors model. Also a model in which both factors are specific can be regarded as a short-run version of the specific-factors model.

4. If a factor, say capital, is sector-specific it is really two factors, since apple capital can't be substituted for butane capital. Thus the specific-factors model can also be thought of as differing from the Heckscher-Ohlin-Samuelson model by having three factors rather than just two, and therefore by having more factors than goods.

5. An increase in the price of a commodity will cause the reward of the factor specific to that sector to rise even more, and the reward of the other specific factor will decline absolutely. Thus the specific factors play the same role as in the Stolper-Samuelson theorem. But the effect on the reward of the mobile factor is ambiguous.

Self-Test

1. Multiple choice: In the specific-factors model, a small change in factor endowments, with commodity prices unchanged:
   1.1. Is impossible, because the factors are specific.
   1.2. Will alter factor prices.
   1.3. Will have no effect on factor prices, by the factor-price equalization theorem.
   1.4. Will have no effect on outputs, because the factors are specific.
   1.5. None of the above.

2. For each of the following, write *S* if the property is a characteristic of the specific-factors model, *H* if it is characteristic of the Heckscher-Ohlin-Samuelson model, *B* if it is characteristic of both models, and *N* if it is characteristic of neither.
   2.1. There are more goods than factors.
   2.2. There are more factors than goods.
   2.3. Relative price changes cause unambiguous changes in all *real* factor rewards.
   2.4. Relative price changes cause unambiguous changes in all *nominal* factor rewards.
   2.5. There are two goods.

Solution to Problem from the Text

3.36 *Show how the effects of an increase in the supply of labor can be described geometrically by a shift of point* H *and the* AA *curve to the left in Figure 3.14 in the textbook. Compare with Figure 3.13(a).*

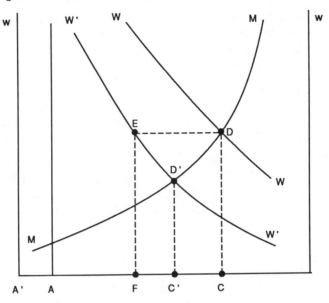

Additional Problems

1. Discuss the usefulness of trying to explain the pattern of comparative advantage on the basis of endowments of specific factors.

2. Suppose that, in contrast to both the Heckscher-Ohlin-Samuelson model and the specific-factors model, *all* factors are sector specific. Discuss the effect of an increase in the price of apples on all factor rewards.

Answers to Self-Test

1. 1.2.

2. 2.1. *N*
   2.2. *S*
   2.3. *H*
   2.4. *H*
   2.5. *H*

9. Possible Explanations of the Leontief Paradox

Basic Ideas

1. This section investigates two minor modifications of the Heckscher-Ohlin-Samuelson model that could conceivably reconcile it with both the casual empiricism that the United States is relatively capital

abundant and the Leontief Paradox (that U.S. import-competing goods are more capital intensive than U.S. exports).

2. A *factor intensity reversal* is present if the technology is such that the commodity which is capital intensive at some factor prices becomes labor intensive at other factor prices. This could potentially explain the paradox, if U.S. imports are labor intensive abroad but capital intensive in the United States.

3. A *demand reversal* is present if a country has a sufficiently pronounced demand (relative to that of the rest of the world) for the good which uses intensively that country's relatively abundant factor, causing the country to import that good.

4. There is a lack of clear empirical evidence that factor intensity reversals do in fact explain the Leontief Paradox, and the evidence seems to indicate that demand reversals do not explain it.

Self-Test

Suppose that a capital-abundant country engages in free trade and specializes completely in the production of the good that, at that country's factor prices, is labor intensive. Which of the following could not account for this state of affairs:

1.1. A demand reversal.
1.2. A factor intensity reversal.
1.3. International differences in technology.

Solutions to Problems from the Text

3.39 *Draw a diagram showing the relation between the wage-rental ratio and the ratio of butane cost (BC) to apple cost (AC) if a factor intensity reversal is present. If the relative factor intensities of the two industries reverse themselves twice.*

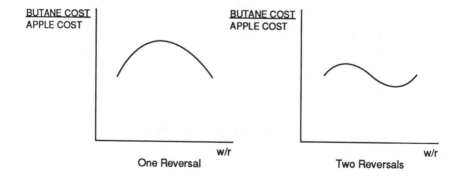

3.40 *If the Leontief Paradox were indeed due to a factor intensity reversal, what would Leontief have found if, instead of calculating the capital and labor used to produce a bundle of U.S. import substitutes, he had calculated the capital and labor actually used in the rest of the world to produce a bundle of U.S. imports? What would he have found if he had performed his actual calculation for the rest of the world rather than for the United States?*

He would not have obtained the paradox in either case.

*3.41 *What can you say about factor-price equalization if a demand reversal is present?*

Factor price equalization must take place with free trade, that is, neither country will specialize in production.

*3.42 *Discuss the factor-price equalization, Rybczynski, and Stolper-Samuelson theorems in the presence of a factor intensity reversal.*

The factor-price equalization theorem no longer applies, but the Rybczynski and Stolper-Samuelson theorems are unaffected, as long as the change in endowments or commodity prices does not carry the country across such a reversal.

Additional Problems

1. It has been suggested that relative factor abundance be determined on the basis of relative autarky factor prices instead of on the basis of physical factor endowments. That is, a country would be classified as labor abundant if, in autarky, w/r were lower in that country than abroad, rather than if K/L were lower in that country than abroad. Discuss how factor intensity reversals and demand reversals affect the Heckscher-Ohlin theorem when this notion of relative factor abundance is used.

2. If we were interested in the factor content of trade rather than its commodity composition, we might revise the Heckscher-Ohlin theorem to state: the capital abundant country will on balance "export" capital and "import" labor, if the factors used to produce its exports are compared to the factors used by the rest of the world to produce that country's imports. Discuss how factor intensity reversals and demand reversals affect this version of the theorem.

3. Discuss the factor-price equalization, Rybczynski, and Stolper-Samuelson theorems in the presence of a demand reversal.

Answer to Self-Test

A demand reversal.

10. Extensions of the Heckscher-Ohlin-Samuelson Model

Basic Ideas

1. This section examines more substantive departures from the Heckscher-Ohlin-Samuelson model. They share the property that trade is still viewed as the consequence of relative factor endowments, and that the model is altered essentially by the addition of more factors and, sometimes, goods.

2. One potential explanation of the Leontief Paradox adds a third factor, *natural resources*, to capital and labor. This could explain the paradox if: capital and natural resources are complements in production; the United States is scarce in natural resources.

3. Another explanation adds *human capital*—the value of education, training, etc. Human capital might either be regarded as a third factor or added to physical capital to obtain a revised measure of total capital.

4. The third explanation looks at *skill groups*. This involves viewing labor as a number of different factors, rather than just one, and allowing many commodities which utilize the various skills.

5. These modifications to the Heckscher-Ohlin-Samuelson model seem to possess considerable explanatory power.

Solutions to Problems from the Text

3.43 *Sometimes human capital is added to physical capital to obtain a measure of total capital, and sometimes the two types of capital are treated as separate factors. Now physical capital itself can take many forms (different types of buildings, different equipment, inventories of different goods), and the form it takes depends upon the sector in which it is employed. If the purpose of the theory is to explain trade in a long-run perspective where capital is completely flexible, how should the two types of capital be treated (added together, or separate)? What difference does it make? Can you think of any reasons to distinguish between human and physical capital but not between forms of the latter?*

The fact that in the long run capital can be reallocated between physical form and human form as well as between different physical types suggests that a single aggregate measure should be used. If this were not done and a study seemed to "explain" trade patterns by relative endowments of the two types of capital (and perhaps other factors), this could simply be a confusion of cause and effect. But one possible reason for distinguishing human capital from physical capital is that their market structures differ: there are markets in which physical capital goods can be bought and sold, but slavery is prohibited.

3.44 *Suppose you were to discover that in nearly all countries wages are generally higher in export industries than in import-competing industries (there is some factual support for this). What would this imply about the empirical relevance of the human capital explanation? Would this cause you to prefer one method of measuring human capital over another?*

This suggests that the wage differentials could reflect something other than human capital, motivating one to try to measure the latter by its cost rather than by wage differentials. It also adds to the reasons for testing the theory with data from trading partners as well as domestic data.

3.45 *Specific skills are due in part to innate ability and in part to training (or human capital). If innate abilities are distributed in about equal proportions in the populations of different countries, should the skill groups and human capital explanations be distinct?*

In principle, no.

*3.46 *Some commodities, because of high transportation costs, do not enter into international trade at all. Personal services are often of this sort. Suppose we alter the basic model by adding a third, nontraded good. Does this change the model in any way beyond increasing the number of goods from two to three? If nontraded goods consist mainly of service industries, what effect would they have on calculations such as Leontief's? Try to deduce the implications of the presence of a nontraded good on the four basic propositions derived from the Heckscher-Ohlin-Samuelson theory.*

Besides increasing the number of goods, adding a nontraded commodity causes tastes to exert a different influence. The quantity of factors to be allocated between the traded goods, in response to international prices, necessarily equals the country's endowment minus the quantity of factors used to produce nontraded goods. But because the latter are nontraded, the quantity produced domestically must equal the quantity demanded, and this depends upon tastes. Thus tastes help to determine the quantity of factors available for the production of traded goods. This is not the case, of course, in the Heckscher-Ohlin-Samuelson model.

11. Alternatives to Factor Endowments

Basic Ideas

1. This section and the next discuss explanations of trade—and of the Leontief Paradox—that are not based on a factor endowments approach, though they may or may not be consistent with such an approach.

2. The alternative explanations considered in this section are all special cases of comparative advantage, even though they differ from the factor-endowments theory, which is also such a special case. The next section, by contrast, considers possibilities that are distinct from comparative advantage.

3. Technological theories assert that a country may have a comparative advantage in the activity of research and development and consequently export a changing mix of new goods, because of the R&D that they embody.

4. Tariffs and other government policies could influence trade enough so that the underlying pattern of comparative advantage is not reflected in actual trade flows.

5. S. B. Linder hypothesized that countries tend to export goods which also have a strong domestic market, because those are the goods a country knows the most about, and that per capita incomes largely determine which goods have strong domestic markets. If so, similarities in per capita incomes would generate trade.

Self-Test

1. Multiple choice: The product cycle refers to:
   1.1. The changing location of production of a particular good over time.
   1.2. The changing location of consumption of a particular good over time.
   1.3. The changing nature of a particular good over time.
   1.4. The changing pattern of comparative advantage over time.
   1.5. A particular type of dog food.

2. True or false: Linder's theory is more concerned with explaining DC-DC trade than DC-LDC trade.

3. Multiple choice: Which of the following ideas is relevant to *both* the product cycle theory and Linder's hypothesis?
   1.1. That differences in tastes are important determinants of the pattern of trade.
   1.2. That innovation is an activity that some countries have a comparative advantage in.
   1.3. That firms can best learn how to produce a good if they have close contact with their customers.
   1.4. All of the above.
   1.5. None of the above.

Additional Problems

1. For each of the explanations discussed in this section, explain either how that explanation could in fact be a manifestation of international differences in relative factor endowments, or else how it has nothing to do with this.

2. What are the two basic assumptions on which Linder's theory is based?

Answers to Self-Test

1. 1.1.

2. True.

3. 1.3.

12. Increasing Returns to Scale and Imperfect Competition

Basic Ideas

1. National economies of scale suggest that countries trade to specialize and reap the rewards of large-scale production. In this case the pattern of trade need not be determinate, or at all significant, so no theory could hope to explain it.

2. International scale economies suggest that intra-industry trade—as opposed to inter-industry trade—could be generated by similarities in relative factor endowments, rather than by differences.

3. Oligopoly provides a basis for inter-industry trade that may either reinforce or counteract the influence of factor endowment differences.

4. Though the theories discussed in this section suggest that intra-industry trade might be negatively related to factor endowment differences, this cannot explain the Leontief Paradox because the latter has to do with the factor content of trade.

Self-Test

1. Multiple choice: In the presence of product differentiation or international economies of scale, international factor mobility and:
   1.1. Inter-industry trade are complements.
   1.2. Intra-industry trade are substitutes.
   1.3. Intra-industry trade are complements.
   1.4. All of the above.
   1.5. None of the above.

2. When do differences in relative factor endowments and the presence of oligopoly tend to promote the *same* pattern of inter-industry trade?

Answers to Self-Test

1. 1.3.

2. When each country's relatively competitive sector makes relatively intensive use of that country's relatively abundant factor.

*13. Exploring Further: Many Goods and Factors

Basic Ideas

1. The four basic propositions derived from the Heckscher-Ohlin-Samuelson model are based upon that model's assumption that there are just two goods and two factors.

2. Empirical work seems to indicate, on the whole, that while relative factor endowments may indeed be crucial determinants of trade patterns, the latter cannot be adequately understood within a two-good, two-factor framework. Thus the relevance of the four basic propositions is intimately related to the degree to which they generalize to models with more goods and factors.

3. This section argues that, although the propositions must be qualified in some significant ways when there are more than two goods and factors, their essential messages retain much validity.

Solutions to Problems from the Text

3.56 *What does the version of the Heckscher-Ohlin theorem deduced in this section imply about the validity of the natural resources explanation of the Leontief Paradox if factor-price equalization takes place?*

If factor price equalization took place and if the United States were abundant in capital and scarce in natural resources, the country would have to be trading an assortment of goods such that the former was on balance exported and the latter imported (in the sense of the factors used in the production of imports and exports), regardless of whether or not those two factors tended to be complementary in individual industries.

3.57 *Go through the reasoning of section *7 of the textbook, as best as you can, if there are three goods and two factors. If there are two goods and three factors.*

This is discussed in section A.5 of Appendix I in the textbook.

14. Review Questions

1. What are the basic assumptions of the Heckscher-Ohlin-Samuelson model?

2. What are the basic results of the Heckscher-Ohlin-Samuelson model?

3. What is the Leontief Paradox? Describe attempts to explain it. What were the most important results to come from these attempts?

4. Discuss the factor-endowment basis of the international trade of the United States.

PART TWO

Further Applications and Extensions of the Pure Theory of International Trade

CHAPTER 4   Tariffs and Trade Theory

1. The Tariff

Basic Ideas

1. A tariff is a tax on imports.

2. Although tariffs take many different forms, their central feature, common to all the forms, is that they cause the relative prices of imports to be higher in domestic markets than on world markets.

Self-Test

Suppose the world price of an imported good rises. Which of the following forms of a tariff on that good would cause the actual degree of protection to rise the most (or fall the least) as a result: specific tariff, ad valorem tariff, variable levy? Which would rise the least (or fall the most)?

Solutions to Problems from the Text

4.1 *In the example of the specific tariff on sparkling wine in the textbook, calculate the equivalent ad-valorem rates on both Asti Spumante and Champagne and compare the two. Suppose instead that sparkling wine is subject to a 10 percent ad-valorem rate. Calculate the equivalent specific tariffs on both products. Suppose that both export prices rise by 50 percent. Calculate the changes in tariff payments in all cases.*

Asti Spumante: $t = (5.17 - 4.00)/4.00 = .29$, or 29 percent.
Champagne: $t = (31.17 - 30.00)/30.00 = .04$, or 4 percent.

4.2 *Explicitly derive expression (4.5) in the textbook from expression (4.4).*

$q = p(1 + t) = p + tp$, so that $q - p = tp$, or, dividing both sides by p, $t = (q - p)/p$.

Additional Problems

1. Countries sometimes subsidize exports. Deduce the differences between a specific subsidy and an ad valorem one. Derive a formula, analogous to (4.5) in the textbook, which shows the relation between q and p produced by an export subsidy of s percent.

2. The text discussed some ways in which it would matter in practice whether a tariff is specific or ad valorem. Try to think of some ways in which a variable levy could in practice differ from the other two.

3. The United States has always had many specific tariffs and many ad valorem tariffs. By contrast, European tariffs became largely specific during the 1920s and have become largely ad valorem since the Second World War. Can you think of any reasons for this change?

4. Examine the actual U.S. tariff structure (see Appendix II of the textbook for data sources). Write a report on U.S. tariffs, covering such aspects as: the different types of tariffs and their relative prevalence, the average size of tariffs, differences between tariffs on different goods, etc.

5. Do the previous problem for Canada. What significant similarities are there between U.S. and Canadian tariffs? Significant differences?

Answer to Self-Test

Rise the most: ad valorem tariff. The least: variable levy.

2. Comparative Advantage and Tariffs

Basic Ideas

1. A tariff causes relative prices to differ between domestic and world markets. As this is just the situation to which the principle of comparative advantage applies, the latter can be used to deduce basic consequences of tariff protection.

2. Tariffs are globally inefficient.

3. A nation levying a tariff suffers a *production cost* in that its GNP is lower, evaluated at actual world prices, as a consequence.

4. A nation levying a tariff suffers a *consumption cost* in that it consumes a collection of goods less desirable than what it could afford to buy, at actual world prices.

5. The production and consumption costs do not imply that a nation necessarily harms itself by levying a tariff, since actual world prices might be different from what they would be in the absence of the tariff.

6. Things to understand: **how the principle of comparative advantage implies the existence of production and consumption costs.**

1. True or false: the production cost of a tariff arises from the fact that protected industries have no incentive to adopt efficient techniques.
2. True or false: the consumption cost arises from the fact that, one way or another, consumers must in the end provide the tariff revenues collected by the government.

Solutions to Problems from the Text

4.5 *Suppose you have the following data for Germany.*

P_B/P_A	B demand	B supply	A demand	A supply
4/3	80	110		30
1	100	100	50	

Suppose the international price of butane is one bushel of apples, and that Germany imports butane with a tariff of 1/3. What is the production cost to Germany in terms of apples? In terms of butane?

$p = 1$ and so $q = 4/3$. Then Germany supplies 110 butane and 30 apples, which are worth 140 apples at $p = 1$. With free trade Germany would supply 100 butane and 50 apples, worth 150 apples. Thus the production cost is 10 apples (or 10 butane).

4.6 *Industries often request tariff protection from foreign competition. But if a tariff protects industry, how can it cause a production cost?*

The protection is for the industry—and its vested interests—but the cost is borne by the economy as a whole.

*4.8 *As in Problem *2.8, 5 labor units are required to produce a unit of either cloth or wine in England, 100 labor units are available, and the English always consume the two goods in equal quantities. Suppose the world price of wine is 1/3 bolts of cloth, and that England imports wine with a 100 percent tariff. What are the production and consumption costs to England?*

The production cost is zero, because England produces 20 cloth both with and without the tariff. With free trade England would trade 5 cloth for 15 wine, consuming 15 of each good. With the tariff England exports 4 cloth for 12 wine, thereby having 16 cloth and 12 wine for consumption. But this is no better than 12 wine and 12 cloth since the two goods are always consumed in equal amounts. Thus the consumption cost of the tariff is in effect 3 wine plus 3 cloth.

Additional Problems

1. The argument in the textbook concluded that a home tariff harmed the world because the MRT_{XM} and MRS_{XM} at home were larger than abroad. Go through the argument again under the assumption that the home and foreign countries both tax their imports.

2. Redraw Figure 4.1 in the textbook to show a country that is better off as a result of levying a tariff, in spite of the production cost.

Answers to Self-Test

1. False.

2. False.

*3. Exploring Further: The Geometry of Tariff Costs

Solutions to Problems from the Text

4.9 *In Figures 4.3 and 4.4 in the textbook, the gray line through E is inside the parallel gray line through N: the combinations of goods equal in value, at domestic prices, to actual production are smaller than the combinations equal in value to actual consumption. Why is this the case? How can you interpret the distance between the two gray lines?*

The amount consumers spend to buy goods exceeds the amount producers receive by the tariff revenue paid to the government. This revenue is equal to the distance between the two lines.

4.10 *Prove that point N in Figures 4.2 and 4.3 in the textbook must lie northwest of M, that is, the consumption distortion of a tariff reduces trade instead of increasing it. On what does your proof depend?*

Since an indifference curve is tangent to the AC line at point M, points between A and M must be intersected by steeper indifference curves, and points between M and C by flatter curves. Since the domestic relative price of imports exceeds the world price, point N must lie at a steeper point on an indifference curve than does M. Thus N must be between A and M.

Additional Problem

Demonstrate that a small country can only harm itself by levying a tariff.

4. Reciprocal Demand and Tariffs

Basic Ideas

1. The imposition of a tariff shifts a country's import demand curve down by a proportion equal to the tariff rate.

2. A tariff will improve a country's terms of trade if that country is large enough to influence world prices.

3. A tariff will increase the relative domestic price of importable goods, unless the country faces a backward-bending foreign export supply curve.

Self-Test

1. What is the Metzler Paradox?

2. Multiple choice: A tariff will bring about a greater improvement in a country's terms of trade:
   2.1. The more elastic its import curve.
   2.2. The less elastic its import curve.
   2.3. The more elastic the rest of the world's export curve.
   2.4. The less elastic the rest of the world's export curve.
   2.5. None of the above.

Solutions to Problems from the Text

4.11 *If you did Problem 2.7 correctly, you obtained the following import demand curve:*

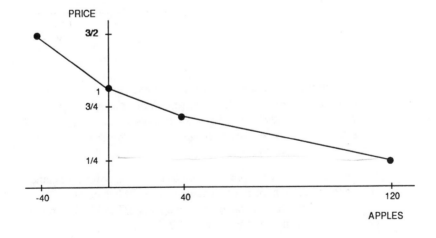

How is it affected by a 50 percent German tariff on apple imports?

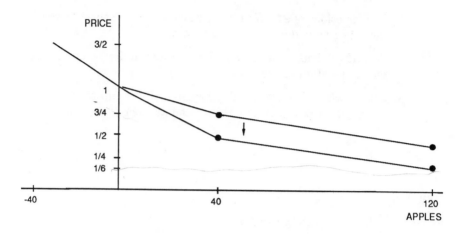

4.12 *If you did Problem 2.6 correctly, you obtained the following export supply curve:*

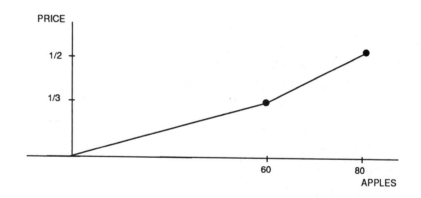

Suppose that France levies no tariff and engages in trade with the Germany of Problem 4.11 above. Show the effect of the German tariff on the trade between the two countries. What is the effect on the terms of trade and on the domestic relative prices in both countries?

With the tariff, France exports 60 apples to Germany for 20 butane. Before the tariff 70 apples were exchanged for 30 butane, so Germany's terms of trade have improved from 3/7 to 1/3. The relative price of an apple in Germany is now 1/2.

4.13 Show how a tariff on imports shifts a country's export supply curve. Use the export supply curve to show the effect of a tariff on international and domestic relative prices. How does a 10 percent French tariff on butane affect the curve in Problem 4.12?

The export supply curve shifts to the left in proportion to the tariff, and it also shifts up in proportion to the tariff.

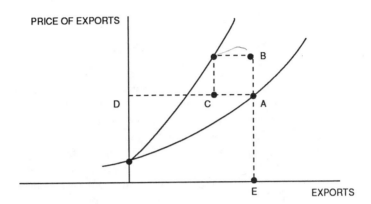

In the above figure, $t = AB/AE = AC/DC$. The other points shift in a similar way.

*4.14 The discussion in the textbook implicitly assumed that the government spends all tariff revenues on exportables. In Figure 4.5(a), for example, domestic citizens pay OECD to the rest of the world, for the import OD, and they pay ABCE to their government as tariff revenue. If some of this revenue, however, is spent on imports, total imports will equal, not OD, but OD plus the imports that are bought with the tariff revenue. Suppose, contrary to the discussion in the text, that the government always spends all tariff revenues on additional imports. Show how a tariff affects the home import demand curve in this case. Under these circumstances, will a tariff still improve the terms of trade? When will it increase the relative domestic price of imports?

The figure below shows a country's free trade import demand curve. Now suppose that the country levies an ad valorem tariff at the rate BC/CD. If the terms of trade are, say, EO, the country would trade at point A. But now, at those same terms of trade, domestic residents face a relative price of imports equal to FO. Thus they purchase OD imports, paying for them with OFBD exportables, of which EFBC is collected by the government as tariff revenue and OECD is exported to pay for the imports.

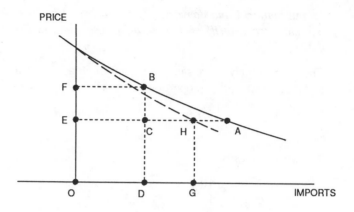

Now, however, the government's revenue is spent on additional imports. At the supposed terms of trade, the tariff revenue of $EFBC$, in terms of exportables, will buy the quantity DG of importables, where $DCHG = EFBC$. Thus the country now trades at point H. Total imports equal OG, of which OD is done by the private sector and DG is done by the government spending its revenues. The quantity $OEHG = OFBD$ is exported to pay for the total imports. Thus the tariff-ridden import demand curve goes through point H rather than point C.

A tariff now shifts the import demand curve down and to the right just enough so that the area under the new curve at any point is just equal to the area under the corresponding point on the original curve. Any inelastic part of the offer curve will now be shifted out, rather than in, as a result of a tariff. This is because, as we move down an import demand curve, the area corresponding to each point becomes larger if the curve is elastic but smaller if it is inelastic. Since the curve in the above figure is elastic, the area determined by A is larger than that determined by B, and therefore larger than that determined by H also, so A must be to the right of H. If the curve had been inelastic, A would have determined a smaller area than H and so been to the left of it.

The following figure shows the effect of a tariff on a country's offer curve if all revenue is spent on importables and if the curve has both elastic and inelastic portions.

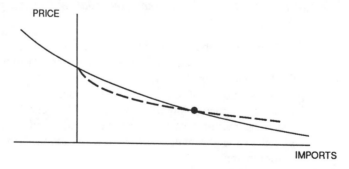

EXTRA QUESTION:

Suppose that a country is trading on the inelastic part of its import demand curve, that it imposes a tariff on imports, and that its government spends all tariff revenues on imports. What is the effect on that country's terms of trade? On its relative domestic price of imports?

Additional Problems

1. Suppose that the France of Problem 4.12 above retaliates against the German tariff by levying its own tariff of 20 percent on imports of butane. Depict this geometrically. What is the effect on the terms of trade and domestic relative prices in both countries? Compare each country's consumption with what it would consume with free trade.

2. Suppose, in Problem *4.14 above, that, instead of spending all tariff revenues on imports, the government spends the revenues exactly as the people would spend them, or, equivalently, that all tariff revenues are redistributed to the population. (This doesn't sound like governments we know, but it could capture the idea that tariff revenues substitute for other taxes that would be levied if the tariff revenues did not exist.) Answer the questions of Problem *4.14 in this case.

Answers to Self-Test

1. A tariff causes the domestic relative price of imports in terms of exports to fall.

2. 2.4.

5. Tariffs and the Factor-Endowments Theory

Basic Ideas

1. A tariff raises the relative domestic price of imports, unless the foreign export supply curve bends back. The application of this conclusion to the basic results of the Heckscher–Ohlin–Samuelson model has implications for the domestic effects of a tariff.

2. The Heckscher–Ohlin theorem implies that a tariff protects the industry that makes relatively intensive use of the country's relatively scarce factor.

3. The Stolper–Samuelson theorem implies that a tariff increases the real reward of the country's relatively scarce factor and lowers that of the country's relatively abundant factor.

4. If factors are specific, a tariff will increase the real reward of those factors specific to the import competing sector and reduce the real reward of those factors specific to the export sector.

Self-Test

1. True or false: A tariff benefits the relatively abundant factor at the expense of the relatively scarce factor.

2. Multiple choice: Assuming that the terms of trade do not significantly improve, a tariff will:
   2.1. Benefit the scarce factor more than it harms the abundant factor.
   2.2. Harm the scarce factor more than it harms the abundant factor.
   2.3. Benefit the abundant factor more than it harms the scarce factor.
   2.4. Benefit the scarce factor less than it harms the abundant factor.
   2.5. Benefit the abundant factor more than it benefits the scarce factor.

Solutions to Problems from the Text

4.15 *On the basis of the discussion in this section of the textbook, which factors of production in the American economy would you expect to favor protection?*

Labor that is not highly skilled and mineral-rich land.

4.17 *What is the effect of a tariff upon the domestic distribution of income if the foreign export supply curve bends back?*

A tariff reduces the relative domestic price of importables thereby lowering the real income of the relatively scarce factor and raising that of the relatively abundant factor.

*4.18 *Deduce how the factor-price equalization theorem would be affected by the presence of a tariff in one or both countries.*

A tariff in either or both countries would prevent relative commodity prices from being equal in the two countries. This means that factor prices could not be made equal by (tariff ridden) trade, even if both countries produce both goods.

Additional Problems

1. Discuss how commercial policy could help explain the differences in agricultural yields shown in Table 3.1 of the textbook. How could changes in such policy help explain the relative wage movements shown in Table 3.2 of the textbook?

2. Discuss the domestic effects of a tariff if the government spends all tariff revenues on imports and if equilibrium occurs on the inelastic part of the home country's import curve. Prepare a table showing the various effects of a tariff under different assumptions about home and foreign elasticities and about government disposal of tariff revenues.

1. False.

2. 2.4.

6. Nontariff Barriers

Basic Ideas

1. There are many distinct tools of protection, but the basic conclusions of tariff theory apply to most of them.

2. A general tax on exports has exactly the same effect on the relative price of imports in terms of exports as does an equal import tariff.

3. A quota is potentially equivalent to a tariff.

Self-Test

1. Multiple choice: A tariff at the rate t is equivalent to:
    1.1 An export subsidy at the rate t.
    1.2 An import subsidy at the rate t.
    1.3 An export tax at the rate t.
    1.4 An export subsidy at the rate $2t$.
    1.5 None of the above.

2. True or false: An import quota is not generally equivalent to a tariff if the government does not in effect sell the quota rights for what they can fetch.

Solutions to Problems from the Text

4.19 *Show how your answers to Problems 4.11 and 4.12 could be duplicated by an appropriate quota.*

Equivalent quotas:

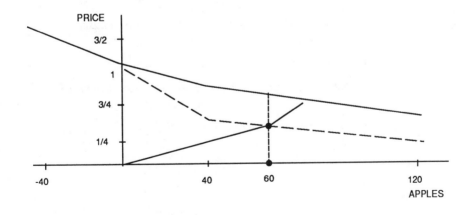

4.21 *The Indian government has established import quotas on many goods used as productive inputs by that country's industry. In some cases these quotas have been allocated among importing firms in proportion to the output capacities of the firms. What is the effect of such an allocation system on economic incentives? Discuss the long-run implications and compare them to those of a tariff.*

Firms would have an incentive to expand output capacity beyond what they actually intend to produce, in order to obtain import quota allotments.

4.22 *Suppose that a certain economy uses three goods: imports, exports, and nontraded goods. There are thus two relative commodity prices: the price of imports in terms of exports and the price of nontraded goods in terms of exports. Show how a tariff on imports affects both relative prices (as equations (4.4) and (4.10) do in the textbook) and do the same for a tax on exports. What do you conclude about the Lerner symmetry theorem?*

A tariff: $Q_X = P_X$, $Q_M = P_M(1 + t)$, and let Q_N denote the domestic price of nontraded goods (there is no world price since the goods are not traded). Let q and p denote the domestic and world relative prices of imports in terms of exports, and let q' and p' denote the relative price of nontraded goods in terms of the domestic price of exports and in terms of the world price of exports, respectively. Then:

$$q = p(1 + t) \text{ and } q' = p'.$$

An export tax: $Q_X(1 + t) = P_X$ and $Q_M = P_M$ so that

$$q = p(1 + t) \text{ and } q' = p'(1 + t).$$

The two policies are no longer equivalent.

4.23 *Consider a quota and its equivalent tariff, as in Figure 4.8 in the textbook. Show how each form of protection causes equilibrium to respond to:*

a. An outward shift of the foreign export supply curve.

b. An outward shift of the home free-trade import demand curve.

a. A shift of the foreign export supply curve, as shown on the facing page:

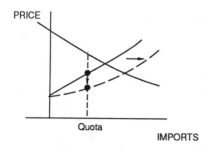

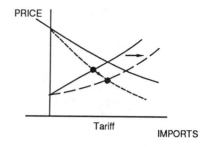

PRICE

PRICE

Quota

IMPORTS

Tariff

IMPORTS

b. A shift of the home free-trade import demand curve:

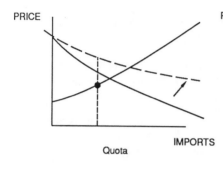

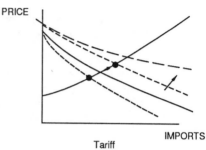

PRICE

PRICE

IMPORTS

Quota

IMPORTS

Tariff

Additional Problems

1. Show how your answers to Problems 4.11 and 4.12 could be duplicated by an appropriate export tax.

2. Suppose that a certain country exercises commercial policy solely through an export quota. Discuss the economic effects, and draw the analog to Figure 4.8 in the textbook. To what extent are import quotas and export quotas related to each other in the way that the Lerner symmetry theorem relates import taxes and export taxes?

3. A certain country imposes a binding quota on imports and auctions off the quota rights. The resulting revenue is then used by the government to purchase additional imports (above the quota amount). Analyze the effects of this policy and compare to the discussion in the text. Compare also to your answer to Problem *4.14.

Answers to Self-Test

1. 1.3.

2. True.

7. Tariffs with Scale Economies and Imperfect Competition

Basic Ideas

1. With national increasing returns to scale, a tariff can inflict a *scale cost*: average costs increase if the tariff causes a good to be produced in several locations rather than in just one, where scale economies could be maximized.

2. If scale economies in some industry are external to the firm, a tariff might benefit the home economy at the expense of the rest of the world by inducing the industry to locate in that country.

3. With an oligopolistic import market, a tariff *shifts profit* to domestic firms from their foreign rivals.

4. With an oligopolistic import market, a tariff harms domestic consumers by its *anticompetitive effect*.

5. In an oligopolistic export market where firms compete by setting quantities, an export subsidy *shifts profit* from foreign firms to domestic firms.

6. In an oligopolistic export market where firms compete by setting quantities, an export subsidy *makes domestic firms compete more* with each other, which reduces their combined profit.

7. In an oligopolistic export market where firms compete by setting *prices*, an export subsidy shifts profit from domestic firms to foreign firms.

Self-Test

1. Multiple choice: The scale cost of a tariff:
   1.1. Is a special case of the production cost.
   1.2. Has the production cost as a special case.
   1.3. Involves producing in the wrong location rather than in too many locations.
   1.4. Involves producing in too many locations rather than in the wrong location.
   1.5. Is a special case of the consumption cost.

2. Multiple choice: Which of the following was shown to give rise to the possibility that a tariff might have a great effect even if it might soon become superfluous?
   2.1. External economies of scale.
   2.2. Internal economies of scale.
   2.3. Oligopoly where firms compete in quantities.
   2.4. Oligopoly where firms compete in prices.
   2.5. None of the above.

Solutions to Problems from the Text

4.24 *The textbook discussed the effects of a tariff if, with free trade, France and Germany both produced butane, which has increasing returns to scale, but only France produced apples, which are subject to constant returns. How does the argument change if initially only Germany produces butane, but both countries produce apples? What do you conclude from this?*

If both countries produce apples and engage in free trade, wages must be the same in the two countries, because otherwise apple producers in the country with the higher wage would be driven out of business. In this case a moderate French tariff would have no effect on French production, though it would subject French consumers to the consumption cost. It could also harm German consumers if it causes butane production to fall, thereby raising costs. But only if the tariff is large enough to be prohibitive could it cause the establishment of a French butane industry.

4.25 *Suppose that the French butane market is a duopoly, with one French firm and one German. What would be the effects of a French tariff on butane if the two firms compete with prices rather than with quantities as discussed in the text?*

The French tariff would shift the German reaction curve out, raising the equilibrium prices charged by both firms, with the German price increasing more than the French. French consumers are worse off. The German firm loses profit, which is shifted to the profit of the French firm and to the tariff revenue of the French government.

Additional Problems

1. The textbook's discussion of external economies of scale considered a free trade equilibrium where France produced both apples and butane, but Germany produced only butane. Compare the welfare of both countries in such an equilibrium with what their welfare would be in autarky. Do the same if the free trade equilibrium instead had France specialized in apple production and Germany producing both goods.

2. What can you say about the Lerner symmetry theorem if both markets are oligopolistic?

3. With oligopoly, could a country ever be tempted to tax imports and exports of the *same* good simultaneously?

4. How would the textbook's discussion of the effects of a tariff in the presence of external economies of scale be altered if the economies were instead *internal* to the firm?

Answers to Self-Test

1. 1.4.

2. 2.1.

8. Review Questions

1. List all the separate welfare effects of a tariff. For each effect, indicate:

   a. *Whose* welfare is influenced and how;

   b. *When* the effect is relevant (size of country, perfect or imperfect competition, type of scale economies, and so on).

2. In what ways does the presence of imperfect competition alter the analysis of the effects of a tariff?

3. What are the implications of comparative advantage for the effects of a tariff?

CHAPTER 5   Commercial Policy

1. Motives for Protection: International Economic Objectives

Basic Ideas

1. This section discusses those reasons that a country might levy tariffs which have to do with the economic relations of that country with the rest of the world.

2. If a country is large enough to influence world prices it can use a tariff to exert its monopoly power and make itself better off. But there is a limit to this, since free trade is better than autarky.

3. The "optimum tariff" is the best a single country can do. It is "optimum" from a purely nationalistic perspective, since it harms the rest of the world more than it benefits the tariff levying country. From a cosmopolitan perspective the optimum tariff is zero.

4. If a country wishes to limit the volume of imports per se, for non-economic reasons, a tariff is an efficient way to do so.

5. In an oligopolistic market, trade policy can be used to shift profit from foreign firms to home firms. It does this by making more aggressive home-firm behavior credible. Depending on circumstances, optimum policy for this purpose could involve either taxes or subsidies.

6. Profit-shifting trade policy in an oligopolistic market is optimal from a nationalistic perspective because it benefits the home country by hurting foreign firms. But it may also be beneficial from a cosmo-politan viewpoint, since an oligopoly is inefficient to begin with.

Self-Test

1. Some primary product exporters attempt to influence their terms of trade by means of an export tax. Write the formula for the optimum export tax.

2. What is the optimum tariff from the point of view of the entire world, rather than from that of the tariff levying country?

3. Multiple choice: An export subsidy:
   3.1. Involves subsidizing foreign consumers.

3.2. May shift profit from domestic firms to foreign firms in an oligopolistic market.
3.3. May shift profit to domestic firms from foreign firms in an oligopolistic market.
3.4. All of the above.
3.5. None of the above.

Solutions to Problems from the Text

5.1 *Some people urged that the United States use the "wheat weapon" against OPEC, that is, force up the price that OPEC must pay for our agricultural exports just as they forced up the price of their oil exports. Discuss the feasibility of such a policy.*

Feasibility is limited by the fact that wheat, and its substitutes, is exported (or can be exported) by many countries.

5.2 *We shall see that tariffs are often second-best policy tools. That is, they are inferior in some ways to alternative methods of achieving whatever goals the tariffs are being used for. Examine each of the three motives discussed in this section to see if you can think of some other, superior policy.*

An optimum tariff policy is first best from the point of view of the levying country, but dominated by international transfer payments from a global perspective. A tariff is a first-best way to limit trade for noneconomic reasons. If an international market is an oligopoly, first-best policy involves eliminating the oligopolistic distortions (in the home market from a nationalistic perspective, and in the world market from a cosmopolitan perspective).

5.3 *The optimum tariff policy* $t = 1/f*$ *would seem to indicate that when on the backward bending part of the foreign export supply curve* $(f* < 0)$, *a subsidy to imports* $(t < 0)$ *is best. But we concluded that tariffs should be* increased *in such a case. Reconcile.*

The formula $t = 1/f*$ holds only if t is actually the optimum tariff; if $f* < 0$ the tariff can't be an optimum one, so the formula is irrelevant.

5.4 *How would the discussion in the textbook of an optimal export subsidy (or tax) change if the home and foreign oligopolists competed in the home market rather than in a foreign one?*

If the home and foreign oligopolists competed in the home market, the effect of commercial policy on domestic consumers would also have to be taken into account. For example, a tariff that shifted profit from the foreign firm to the domestic firm would increase home welfare by doing so. But if it raised prices, it would make domestic consumers worse off. Thus the tariff would have a *distributional* effect (helping firms partly at the expense of consumers), and the overall effect on national welfare would be the sum of these two component effects.

Additional Problems

1. Draw Figure 5.1 in the textbook as it would appear if the home country were small in world markets.

2. Suppose that the home and foreign countries both pursue optimum tariff policies, and that each country ends up imposing a tariff that is optimum, given the tariff of the other country. What is the relationship between the home domestic relative price of imports, q, and the relative price, q^*, of the same two goods prevailing in the foreign country? Draw the analog to Figure 5.1 in the textbook.

3. Suppose that the foreign export curve shifts outwards, as a result either of a reduction in foreign tariffs or of economic growth abroad. Show geometrically what this implies about an optimum tariff levied by the home country.

Answers to Self-Test

1. $t = 1/f^*$.

2. Zero.

3. 3.4.

2. Motives for Protection: Internal Economic Objectives

Basic Ideas

1. Governments use tariffs to raise revenue. Because they are relatively simple taxes to administer, tariffs are frequently important revenue sources in LDCs. They are no longer so important in most DCs, although they were historically.

2. Because they influence relative domestic prices, tariffs can be used to deal with external economies, market imperfections, and other distortions. But because they introduce distortions of their own, tariffs are "second best," relative to more direct measures. The infant industry argument—that temporary tariffs are necessary to establish an industry which will be viable on its own in the long run—is an important example of this class of motives.

3. Because they influence consumption and production, tariffs can be used to attain noneconomic objectives with regard to these two activities. But again they are in principle second-best methods.

4. Terms to understand: **external economies and diseconomies, domestic distortions, second best.**

1. True or false: "External economies" refer to cost reductions that can be achieved if goods are produced abroad rather than at home.

2. True or false: Tariffs are "second best" because they are usually imposed for questionable motives.

3. True or false: Although tariffs are in principle a second-best way of raising government revenue, alternative methods could in practice be so difficult to administer that tariffs are in fact best.

Solutions to Problems from the Text

5.5 *This section showed that a tariff was a second-best way of attaining a noneconomic objective because other methods can do the same without the consumption cost. Does this argument apply to the motive of trade limitation for noneconomic reasons discussed in the previous section of the textbook? What is the essential difference between the two motives?*

With trade limitation for noneconomic reasons, the policy objective is to discriminate against imported goods, and the tariff is a direct way of doing this. If the objective is instead to achieve a production target or a consumption target, a tariff is an indirect method and the discrimination against imported goods which it introduces is an unnecessary side effect.

5.6 *Is the tariff a second-best method of raising government revenue? If so, what methods are better?*

Yes. Lump-sum taxes, for example, do not introduce the distortions that tariffs do.

Additional Problems

1. The government would like to reduce the domestic consumption of horned winglaks which, as all the world knows, are imported but also produced domestically. For this purpose a tariff on horned winglaks is under consideration. Would a consumption tax be preferable? Why? If a tariff is cheaper to administer than is a consumption tax, how much cheaper must it be for the tariff to be as good a method as a consumption tax?

2. Based on your investigation of U.S. tariffs for Additional Problem 4 on page 66, do any U.S. tariffs seem to be due to any of the motives discussed in this section of the textbook?

3. Based on your investigation of Canadian tariffs for Additional Problem 5 on page 66, do any Canadian tariffs seem to be due to any of the motives discussed in this section of the textbook?

1. False.
2. False.
3. True.

3. Motives for Protection: Income Distribution

Basic Ideas

1. Because tariffs influence relative domestic prices, they can be used to alter the domestic distribution of income.

2. In the long run a tariff will raise the real earnings of a country's relatively scarce factor and reduce the real earnings of the relatively abundant factor.

3. In the short run factors can be quite industry specific. In this case tariffs raise the earnings of factors employed in the import-competing sector and lower the real earnings of factors employed in the export sector.

4. A tariff is again a second-best method: the gainers gain less than the losers lose.

5. Terms to understand: **specific factors, long run vs. short run.**

Self-Test

1. Multiple choice: In the long run the owner of a certain factor of production will be better off if:
   1.1. Not very much of her income is spent on imports.
   1.2. That factor is the one which the export sector employs intensively.
   1.3. She uses her factor in the import competing sector.
   1.4. Not very much of her income is spent on exportables.
   1.5. None of the above.

2. Multiple choice: In the short run the owner of a certain factor of production will be better off if:
   2.1. Not very much of his income is spent on imports.
   2.2. That factor is the one which the export sector employs intensively.
   2.3. He uses his factor in the import competing sector.
   2.4. Not very much of his income is spent on exportables.
   2.5. None of the above.

5.7 *The optimum tariff argument supplies a motive where the tariff is a first-best tool from a nationalistic perspective. But from a cosmopolitan perspective is it a first-best method for redistributing income between countries? Why? If it is not, what methods are better and why?*

A tariff is second best from a cosmopolitan perspective because it reduces world income, whereas direct international transfer payments would not, and are thereby first best.

Additional Problems

1. The nation of Upper Arrogancia finds its import competing industries mired in a worldwide recession, and its leaders are considering a dramatic rise in tariff protection as a method of stimulating employment in the import sector. But they are concerned about the possibility of foreign retaliation. What circumstances would make retaliation more likely? Less likely?

2. If a tariff causes losers to lose more than gainers gain, how could a democracy ever end up imposing tariffs?

Answers to Self-Test

1. 1.5.

2. 2.3.

*4. Exploring Further: The Second-Best Nature of the Tariff

Basic Ideas

1. A tariff is a second-best method of dealing with domestic distortions because it cures the latter by introducing distortions of its own.

2. A small tariff will introduce less harmful distortions than it neutralizes and so is better than free trade.

3. It never pays to levy a tariff large enough to completely neutralize the domestic distortion.

4. An intermediate tariff could be better, or worse, than free trade.

Solutions to Problems from the Text

5.8 *This section suggested two possible first-best ways of dealing with the trade association example of a distortion. Are those two ways equivalent? What would determine which should be used?*

The differences are in implementation. A production subsidy would have to be financed by a tax of some sort, and so requires the administrative costs of the tax cum subsidy plus any distortions introduced by the tax. Breaking down the trade association would presuppose some policy of economic intervention.

5.10 *Formulate analogs of this section's four conclusions that apply to the use of a tariff to improve the terms of trade.*

If a country is able to influence its terms of trade, a tariff is a first-best way of doing so (from that country's point of view; it is a second-best method of international income redistribution from a global standpoint). A small tariff is definitely better for such a country than is free trade, but a prohibitive tariff (that is, a retreat into autarky) is worse than free trade. An intermediate tariff may be either better or worse than no tariff at all.

Additional Problems

1. Go through the analysis of this section in detail if the motivation for tariff policy is not a domestic distortion, but rather a desire to limit domestic consumption of importables for noneconomic reasons.

2. Prove each of the four conclusions of this section of the textbook without using community indifference curves.

5. Effective Protection

Basic Ideas

1. A tariff on an intermediate good, such as steel, raises the cost of goods, such as automobiles, that use that intermediate good. Thus a tariff on steel reduces the degree of protection given to the activity of producing automobiles.

2. The effective rate of protection of a particular activity measures the net effect of a country's tariff structure on that activity.

3. Industrial countries typically levy higher taxes at later stages of production, resulting in even higher effective rates at those later stages.

4. Be sure to understand: **how to derive and to use the effective rate formula; the difference between nominal and effective tariff rates.**

Self-Test

1. True or false: effective rates of protection are always at least as high as nominal rates, and often very much higher.

2. True or false: the fact that many effective tariff rates are much higher in industrial countries than are the (typically modest) nominal rates indicates that the production and consumption costs of those countries' tariff structures are actually significantly greater than the nominal rates would seem to indicate.

Solutions to Problems from the Text

5.11 *Suppose that shoes have a 25 percent nominal tariff rate, leather a 15 percent rate, and two-thirds of the cost of a pair of shoes is due to the leather they contain, and one-third to value added. What is the effective rate of protection of the activity of making shoes from leather?*

The effective rate of protection of making shoes from leather: $e = .25 + (.25 - .15)[(2/3)/(1/3)] = .25 + .2 = .45$. Thus the effective rate is 45 percent.

5.12 *Suppose that, in a refinery, a_o barrels of crude oil, a_c tons of coal, and a_m units of materials are combined with value added to yield b_g gallons of gasoline and b_a gallons of aviation fuel. If P_o, P_c, P_m, P_g, and P_a denote the world prices of oil, coal, materials, gasoline, and aviation fuel respectively, if t_o, t_c, t_m, t_g, and t_a denote the corresponding nominal tariff rates, derive a formula, analogous to (5.4) in the textbook, for the effective rate of protection of refining, e_R.*

e_R equals:

$$\left[\left(\frac{P_g b_g}{Q}\right)t_g + \left(\frac{P_a b_a}{Q}\right)t_a\right] + \left(\left[\left(\frac{P_g b_g}{Q}\right)t_g + \left(\frac{P_a b_a}{Q}\right)t_a\right]\right.$$

$$\left. - \left[\left(\frac{P_o a_o}{[Q-v]}\right)t_o + \left(\frac{P_c a_c}{[Q-v]}\right)t_c + \left(\frac{P_m a_m}{[Q-v]}\right)t_m\right]\right)\left(\frac{[Q-v]}{v}\right)$$

where $Q = P_g b_g + P_a b_a$, so that

$$Q - v = P_o a_o + P_c a_c + P_m a_m.$$

*5.13 *Consider the example of steel and autos in the textbook. Gross output, denoted X_A and X_S for autos and steel respectively, refers to the total output of an industry. Net output (Y_A and Y_S) refers to gross output less that part of output used as an input in other industries (that is, that part of gross output available for consumption or export). Thus, $Y_A = X_A$ and $Y_S = X_S - aX_A$. Chapter 1 of the textbook showed that relative* *commodity prices equal the marginal rate of transformation between any two goods that are actually produced. Show that this refers to the MRT between net outputs. Will the ratio of values added per unit equal the MRT between gross outputs? Why? What do you conclude about the significance of effective rates of protection?*

Let *MRTN* denote the marginal rate of transformation of steel for automobiles between net outputs, and let *MRTG* denote that between gross outputs. Net output is what a country actually has available to consume or to sell. Thus if $P_a > P_s MRTN$, where P_s and P_a denote the respective prices of steel and automobiles, the country (or a firm) could increase its income by producing less steel and more automobiles. Thus $p = MRTN$, where $p = P_a/P_s$. Now, with the assumed production structure, $MRTN = MRTG - a$. Thus $MRTG = MRTN + a = p + a = (P_a + aP_s)/P_s$, which is the ratio of values added per unit.

Additional Problems

1. In Table 5.2 in the textbook, suppose that the output of each stage of processing is produced only from value added plus the output of the immediately preceding stage (that is, stage 3 uses value added plus stage 2 output, but does not directly use any stage 1 or stage 4 output). For each stage, calculate the shares of total cost accounted for by value added and by intermediate inputs.

2. In the preceding problem, suppose that stages 3 and 4 of processing are performed in a single plant. Calculate the effective rate of protection accorded to the activity of that plant.

Answers to Self-Test

1. False.

2. False.

6. The Political Economy of Tariffs

Basic Ideas

1. Since tariffs are only second best with regard to most of the motives examined, it is curious that protection has been so widespread.

2. Protection is often justified on the basis of fallacious economic arguments.

3. Since protection generally helps some groups while hurting others, it has often been examined in terms of pressure group politics.

4. Studies of the characteristics of protected industries have had mixed success, but there is some evidence that industrial nations tend to protect most heavily the industries that use unskilled labor most intensively.

Self-Test

1. What is the "scientific tariff"?
2. True or false: The industrial nations tend to give relatively high protection to industries making relatively intensive use of unskilled labor.

Answers to Self-Test

1. A tariff equal to the excess of domestic production cost above foreign production cost.

2. True.

7. Commercial Policies after the Second World War

Basic Ideas

1. The General Agreement on Tariffs and Trade (GATT) is the primary vehicle for international cooperation on commercial policy.

2. The basic GATT agreement prohibits quantitative restrictions on trade and mandates use of the Most Favored Nation (MFN) clause, though there are exceptions.

3. GATT has also sponsored a series of multilateral tariff reduction negotiations, and it helps to settle trade disputes between nations.

4. The GATT rounds of tariff reductions have reduced tariffs on the trade of manufactured goods among industrial nations to historic lows.

5. There has been relatively little success in liberalizing agricultural trade, trade involving the LDCs, and nontariff trade barriers.

6. The most recent GATT negotiations, the Tokyo Round, developed a set of Codes of Conduct regarding nontariff barriers.

7. The forthcoming round of GATT negotiations will be the first to deal with trade in services and counterfeiting, both of great concern to the United States.

8. In recent years there has been an apparent resurge of protectionism in the DCs, emphasizing the application of discretionary nontariff trade barriers in response to the demands of special interests.

Self-Test

1. What does GATT stand for?

2. What did ITO stand for?

3. Multiple choice: the GATT rounds of tariff negotiations:
   3.1. Were a major advance because they abandoned the reciprocity principle emphasized earlier by the United States.
   3.2. Were bilateral rather than multilateral, thus allowing the negotiators to get down to the nitty gritty.
   3.3. Focused upon across the board reductions, rather than item by item negotiations, starting with the Kennedy Round.
   3.4. None of the above.
   3.5. All of the above.

4. True or false: Despite the threats, both real and imagined, of the "new protectionism," tariffs on the trade between the industrial nations remain by and large at historically low levels.

Answers to Self-Test

1. General Agreement on Tariffs and Trade.

2. International Trade Organization.

3. 3.3.

4. True.

8. Tools of the New Protectionism

Basic Ideas

1. International agreements (notably the GATT) restrict the ability of nations to conduct trade policy by the comprehensive revision of tariff laws, the historical method. Thus various discretionary methods are more important.

2. Prominent U.S. measures, also used by many other nations, include: the escape clause (safeguard provisions), anti-dumping and counter-vailing duty laws, and measures to deal with unfair trade practices.

3. Trade Adjustment Assistance, the national security clause and provisions for agricultural trade measures are other U.S. policy tools.

4. Things to understand: **the workings of the various measures.**

1. Multiple choice: the escape clause:
   1.1. Allows countries to escape from foreign tariffs, if they are too high.
   1.2. Safeguards domestic export industries from the threat of a sudden increase in foreign tariffs.
   1.3. Provides for financial relief to domestic firms and workers hurt by foreign tariffs.
   1.4. None of the above.
   1.5. All of the above.

2. True or false: In practice, the measures discussed in this section have often been powerful influences inducing the negotiation of "voluntary" export restraints.

3. What does TAA stand for?

4. Why do you think that the countervailing duty law generates little government revenue, even when it is rigorously enforced?

Answers to Self-Test

1. 1.4.

2. True.

3. Trade Adjustment Assistance.

4. Because when countervailing duties seem likely to be imposed, foreign governments often drop their subsidies, so that the latter will not simply be appropriated by the U.S. government.

9. Review Questions

1. Compare and contrast U.S. tariff history with that of Canada. What are the major similarities and differences? Explain each.

2. List the major reasons for protection. For each, state who gains and who loses, and state whether a tariff is first best or not, from the perspective of the tariff-levying country and from that of the world as a whole.

3. Discuss the "new protectionism." What is it and how does it differ from the old? What are its most important tools?

4. Discuss attempts since the Second World War to reach multilateral agreements on trade policy.

CHAPTER 6   International Factor Movements

1. The Basic Theory of International Factor Movements

Basic Ideas

1. This section examines aspects of international factor movements common to all factors.

2. If factors of production are mobile internationally, absolute advantage replaces comparative advantage as the basic determinant of production and trade patterns.

3. If international trade is due to differences in relative factor endowments across countries, trade and factor movements are substitutes.

4. If trade is due to some other cause, trade and factor movements are likely to be complements.

5. Factor movements and intra-industry trade are complements.

Self-Test

1. Multiple choice: The pattern of international commodity trade is determined by:
   1.1. Absolute advantage if factors are internationally mobile and comparative advantage if they are not.
   1.2. Absolute advantage if factors are not internationally mobile and comparative advantage if they are.
   1.3. Comparative advantage in either case.
   1.4. Absolute advantage in either case.
   1.5. None of the above.

2. True or false: In the Heckscher-Ohlin-Samuelson model, if international capital mobility, as well as trade, is free, wage rates will become equalized across countries.

3. Multiple choice: International labor mobility can be expected to:
   3.1. Increase inter-industry trade and reduce intra-industry trade.
   3.2. Increase both inter-industry and intra-industry trade.
   3.3. Reduce both inter-industry and intra-industry trade.
   3.4. Increase intra-industry trade and reduce inter-industry trade.
   3.5. None of the above.

Solutions to Problems from the Text

6.1 *In the simple Ricardian example of Table 6.1 and Table 6.2 in the textbook, is it meaningful to talk of the French and German production possibility frontiers once labor becomes internationally mobile? What about the world frontier? Draw such a curve, if you can, and compare it with Figure 1.2(a) in the textbook. (Assume, as in chapter 1, that, initially, France has 600 workers and Germany 500.)*

The world frontier:

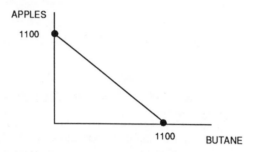

6.2 *Our discussion of the simple Ricardian model tacitly assumed that French and German laborers were identical and that the productivity differences in Table 6.1 in the textbook reflected differences in climate. Suppose, instead, that Table 6.1 shows each country's labor productivity* at home, *but that three French laborers are always required to do the same work that could be done in the same country by one German worker (thus two German workers can produce one unit of butane in France, and so forth). Derive the world production possibility frontier in this case. Describe who produces what, where, at various points along this curve.*

The world frontier:

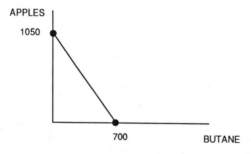

6.3 *In Problem 6.2, suppose that everyone in the world always consumes equal amounts of apples and butane. Fully describe international equilibrium.*

In equilibrium the world produces 420 apples and 420 units of butane. French workers in France produce 300 apples, German workers in France produce the remaining 120 apples, and German workers in Germany produce the 420 units of butane.

*6.4 *How is our discussion of international factor mobility and the Heckscher-Ohlin-Samuelson model affected if, before either factor is internationally mobile, the two countries are separated by a factor intensity reversal?*

Once either factor becomes mobile the two countries will not be separated by a factor intensity reversal, since they will have the same factor prices. Thus such a reversal can affect only the pre-factor mobility situation, which we studied in chapter 3 of the textbook.

*6.5 *Discuss how our treatment of factor mobility and the Heckscher-Ohlin-Samuelson model changes if technology is different in the two countries.*

International mobility of one factor, say capital, will still cause its rent to be equalized across countries, but wages need not be. Therefore free trade in goods and one factor no longer renders international mobility of the second factor superfluous. If both factor prices are equalized, as they would be if both factors were mobile, the international trade of goods would not be superfluous but would proceed on the basis of absolute advantage.

*6.6 *Figure 3.6 in the textbook used the Rybczynski theorem to show the effect of economic growth on international trade. In similar fashion, depict the effects of international factor movements on international trade.*

The basic argument is the same, since an inflow of capital is just one particular cause of the growth of a country's capital stock. The main difference is that capital which flows into one country necessarily flows out of the other country from which it came, so that the shift of one import curve in the figure should now be accompanied by an opposite shift of the other country's export curve.

*6.7 *Suppose two countries, each resembling the specific factors model, engage in free trade. Discuss the results, for factor price equalization and other possible properties, if the intersectorally mobile factor, labor, also becomes internationally mobile. What happens if, instead, one of the sector specific factors becomes internationally mobile (but remains intersectorally immobile)? Discuss how international factor mobility can substitute for intersectoral factor mobility.*

Suppose that two countries engage in free trade, with all the assumptions of the Heckscher-Ohlin-Samuelson model holding except that one factor, say capital, is not mobile across industries. If labor, the intersectorally mobile factor, also becomes mobile across countries, wages will become equal in the two nations. *This means that the rent of each type of capital must also be equal across countries.* To see why this is so, suppose that instead the rent of apple capital were higher in Germany than in France. Since the German apple industry would have to pay exactly the same as the French apple industry for labor and more for capital its costs would necessarily be higher. Therefore German apple producers would be unable to compete with the French and would be driven out of business. This would leave German apple capital unemployed, since it is unable to move into the butane industry. Thus the rent paid to German apple capital would fall until it equaled the rent paid to French apple capital, so that German apple producers could stay in business and employ the German apple capital.

Thus international mobility of the intersectorally mobile factor causes factor price equalization. The pattern of trade would then be determined by the two countries' relative endowments of apple capital and butane capital.

Suppose now that it is instead one of the *specific* factors that is internationally mobile. Imagine that apple capital can freely move between France and Germany, but must always be used by an apple firm. Labor and butane capital remain immobile between countries. The rent received by apple capital will therefore become equal in the two countries. Then the wage must also be equal, if both countries continue to produce apples. This is because, if wages were in fact unequal, the country with the higher wage could not possibly compete in the world apple market, with both countries paying the same rent for apple capital. By the same reasoning, the fact that wages are equal in the two countries requires the rent of butane capital to be equal also. Thus all factor prices are again equalized, if both countries continue to produce apples. It is possible, however, that all of the now internationally mobile apple capital will locate in one country, causing the other country to specialize in butane. In such a case factor prices need not be equal. This will in fact happen if the two countries' relative endowments of labor and butane capital are sufficiently dissimilar. If they are not, factor price equalization must ensue.

The general conclusion, then, is that the international mobility of one specific factor plus international trade in goods produces factor price equalization, and completely substitutes for mobility of the other two factors, provided that relative endowments of those two factors are not too different across countries. International mobility of the intersectorally mobile factor, on the other hand, is (if accompanied by free trade in goods) a perfect substitute for international mobility of the other two factors regardless of relative factor endowments.

Additional Problems

1. Suppose that we modify the Heckscher-Ohlin-Samuelson model by assuming that the French apple industry is uniformly more efficient than the German (that is, any combination of capital and labor can produce more apples in France than the same combination could produce in Germany) and that the German butane industry is uniformly more efficient than the French. Initially the two countries are equally capital abundant (they have the same endowment of capital per worker), their tastes are identical, and apple production is the

capital intensive industry. Starting from a state of autarky, the two countries begin free trade in both goods and also allow the free international movement of capital. What will happen?

2. In the preceding problem, is the amount of international trade greater or less than what it would be if capital were not internationally mobile? If an economist were to apply Leontief's procedure to post trade data what would she find? What do you conclude from all this?

Answers to Self-Test

1. 1.1.

2. True.

3. 1.4.

2. Labor Migration

Basic Ideas

1. This section examines aspects of international factor movements characteristic of labor.

2. The "brain drain" refers to the international movement of skilled labor. Such people bring their human capital with them, so that in effect two factors simultaneously move. This has been of concern primarily to the source countries. The brain drain limits the ability of countries to undertake independent taxation and social policies.

3. The temporary migration of unskilled workers is the most prominent contemporary form of international labor mobility.

4. This migration is sometimes legal, as in the case of European guest worker systems, and sometimes illegal, as with much of the temporary migration of Caribbean and Central American workers into the United States.

5. Countries who welcome temporary unskilled migrants do so in order to help shield themselves from the business cycle and other changes, and in order to preserve their own labor-intensive industries.

6. The U.S. immigration law has recently been revised in an attempt to deal better with the problem of illegal immigration. Notable changes include penalties for firms that knowingly employ illegal immigrants and amnesty for migrants that had been in the country for an extended period.

7. Be sure you can explain: **the brain drain, guest worker systems.**

Solution to Problem from the Text

6.8 *In chapter 5 we saw that a small tariff would improve the welfare of any country large enough to influence its terms of trade.
How is this argument affected if the importable sector is relatively intensive in the use of unskilled (migrant) labor, and if
the incomes of such migrants are not counted as part of national
welfare?*

The Stolper-Samuelson theorem implies that the real incomes of migrants will rise while that of the other factor falls. Thus, if migrant
incomes are not counted as part of national welfare, the country would
be worse off, despite the improvement in its terms of trade.

Additional Problems

1. Find some countries with significant income in the form of remittances from migrants working abroad (see Appendix II of the textbook
for data sources). Why do you think that remittances are so important
for these particular countries? Where do you think that most of their
migrants have gone?

2. The textbook discussed several instances where labor mobility and
trade seem to be substitutes. The preceding section of the textbook,
however, pointed out that sometimes trade and factor mobility can be
complementary. Think of some concrete cases where this is perhaps
true with regard to labor.

3. International Capital Movements

Basic Ideas

1. This section examines aspects of international factor movements
characteristic of capital.

2. International capital movements refer to borrowing and lending between countries, not to the international trade of capital goods.

3. Because a country pays for what it buys from the rest of the world,
the capital balance and the current balance always sum to zero.

4. In the early 1980s, the United States was the nation with the largest
net creditor position in the world. But then very large current account
deficits transformed the country into the world's largest debtor in just
a few years.

5. Be sure you can explain the following: **capital inflow and outflow,
current balance, capital balance, stocks vs. flows, official
transactions, long term vs. short term, direct vs. portfolio
investment.**

Self-Test

1. The nation of Polonia has thus far neither a borrower nor a lender been. In 1990 Polonia buys $1 billion of foreign bonds, in 1991 Polonia receives 10 percent interest on the bonds, and in 1992 the issuer of the bonds defaults. No other capital movements take place. What is Polonia's trade balance in 1990, 1991, and 1992?

2. If the foreign subsidiary of an American firm issues bonds to its parent, is it portfolio or direct investment?

Solutions to Problems from the Text

6.9 *For each of the following transactions, tell, from the point of view of each country, whether the transaction contributes to the current balance or the capital balance and, if the latter is the case, what type of capital movement it is.*

  a. *New Yorkers use checks drawn on a New York bank to buy bonds from a Canadian corporation.*

  b. *The Soviet Union sends oil to Germany in exchange for oil-drilling equipment.*

  c. *The Soviet Union, in exchange for oil-drilling equipment, promises to send Japan 100 million barrels of oil from the new well in five years.*

  d. *An American firm issues six-month commercial paper in London to finance the purchase of a British department store.*

  e. *You use a check drawn on a Philadelphia bank to buy a vacation home on the Mediterranean.*

  a. N.Y. checks: short-term capital; Canadian bonds: long-term (portfolio) capital.

  b. Current transaction (trade).

  c. Equipment: current transaction (trade); promise of future oil: capital transaction.

  d. Commercial paper: short-term capital; purchase of department store: long-term capital.

  e. Check: short-term capital; house: long-term capital.

6.10 *In section 2 of the textbook we saw that remittances from natives working abroad are important sources of income for some countries. How do you think that such payments fit into the scheme of Figure 6.3 in the text?*

  The current balance.

Additional Problems

1. If the capital balance and the current balance must always just cancel, how can trade and capital movements ever possibly be complements, as section 1 of the textbook said they sometimes are?

2. The textbook argued that Walras's Law implies that the current and capital balances always sum to zero. Why are labor movements not also included?

Answers to Self-Test

1. 1990: +$1 billion; 1991: –$100 million; 1992: 0.

2. Direct.

*4. Exploring Further: Intertemporal Trade

Basic Ideas

1. The two-commodity trade models developed in Part One of the text can be used to study intertemporal trade if the goods are thought of as "present goods" and "future goods."

2. The relative price of present goods in terms of future goods is one plus the rate of interest.

3. A net import of present goods in exchange for future goods constitutes a present current-account deficit (or capital-account surplus).

4. Our earlier trade theory (such as that of tariffs) can be applied in a straightforward way to analyze the current account.

Self-Test

1. Multiple choice: The application of the principle of comparative advantage to intertemporal trade predicts that, when international capital movements are allowed:
   1.1. The country with the higher autarky interest rate will become a lender.
   1.2. The country with the higher autarky interest rate will become a borrower.
   1.3. The country with the higher autarky interest rate will develop a current-account surplus.
   1.4. The country with the higher autarky interest rate will become poorer.
   1.5. None of the above.

2. Suppose a country with a current-account deficit imposes a tariff on the purchase of foreign goods. What happens if the analog of the *Metzler paradox* holds?

Solutions to Problems from the Text

6.11   *Draw Figure 6.4 as it would appear if France were in the international equilibrium depicted in Figure 6.5. Do the same for Germany.*

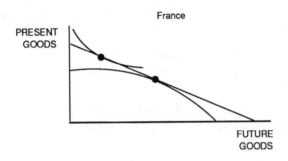

France

PRESENT GOODS

FUTURE GOODS

6.12   *Suppose that Figures 6.4 and 6.5 are generated by the Heckscher-Ohlin-Samuelson model of chapter 3, where labor and land are the two primary factors, present goods are relatively labor intensive, and (as in the HOS model) both of these primary factors are immobile internationally. Discuss the meaning of the four basic HOS theorems in this context. Contrast this with the conclusions reached in section 1 of this chapter, where one of the primary factors was internationally mobile, and both goods were "present" goods.*

The Heckscher-Ohlin theorem, for example, would predict that the relatively labor abundant country would experience (in the present) a capital-account surplus and the land abundant country would experience a capital-account deficit.

*6.13   *What happens to the equilibrium in Figure 6.5 if France imposes a tariff on the import of German goods, and spends the proceeds on future goods? Does it matter if France taxes exports instead? Suppose it taxes the sale of assets to foreigners? The payment of interest to foreigners?*

A tariff on German goods would shift the French current-account demand curve down, producing a fall in the rate of interest and a reduction in the French capital-account surplus. The equivalent export tax would be a tax on promises to repay in the future, not a tax on the export of present goods.

Answers to Self-Test

1. 1.1.

2. The domestic rate of interest and the foreign rate of interest both fall.

5. The Transfer Problem

Basic Ideas

1. The transfer problem is concerned with the short-term effects of a payment from one country to another. The payment could be due to a loan, a gift, or reparations. The perspective is short term in the sense that neither the cause of the payment nor any ultimate effects on productive capacity are considered.

2. A transfer is *undereffected* or overeffected as it generates a trade surplus for the paying country that is less than or greater than the amount of the transfer itself.

3. A transfer may generate a *secondary burden*, or a secondary benefit, for the paying country by causing the terms of trade to move against it, or in its favor.

4. The paying country will experience a secondary burden, and the transfer will be undereffected, according to whether or not the sum of the home and foreign marginal propensities to import exceed unity or not.

Self-Test

1. True or false: A transfer is said to be undereffected if spending in the recipient country fails to rise by the full amount of the transfer.

2. Multiple choice: Atlantis is making a transfer payment to Utopia, and in Atlantis the marginal propensity to save is 1/3 and the marginal propensity to import is 1/4. Atlantis will suffer a secondary burden if in Utopia
   2.1. The marginal propensity to save is 1/3.
   2.2. The marginal propensity to import is 3/4.
   2.3. The marginal propensity to export is –3/5.
   2.4. The marginal propensity to consume is 2/3.
   2.5. None of the above.

Solutions to Problems from the Text

6.16 *Suppose that the French marginal propensity to import is one-fifth and the German is three-tenths. France makes a transfer payment of $10 billion to Germany.*

   a. Will the transfer be over- or undereffected, and what will happen to the terms of trade?

   b. Calculate the exact amount by which, at the initial terms of trade, the transfer is not effected. What is the induced capital movement (C')?

   c. Calculate the value of the excess demand for French importables produced by the transfer at the original terms of trade. What is the excess demand for French exportables?

Since the sum of the marginal propensities to import = $(1/5) + (3/10)$ = $1/2 < 1$, the transfer will be undereffected and the French terms of trade will deteriorate. The transfer will be undereffected by $(1/5)10 + (3/10)10 = \$5$ billion, which therefore also equals the induced capital movement. The excess demand for French importables (and excess supply of French exportables) will also equal \$5 billion.

6.17 *The Heckscher-Ohlin-Samuelson model studied in chapter 3 of the textbook assumed that both countries had identical tastes. How are our conclusions about the transfer problem affected if this assumption is accurate? What do you conclude about the influence of international taste similarities on the ability of the world economy to accommodate transfers?*

Identical tastes in the Heckscher–Ohlin–Samuelson sense imply that that $m = 1 - m^*$, or $m + m^* = 1$, so that all transfers will be exactly affected.

*6.19 *Discuss how our analysis of the transfer problem should be amended if, in both the paying and receiving countries, there is, in addition to importables and exportables, a class of non-tradable goods.*

Suppose the home country makes a transfer payment of T abroad. Let m and n denote, respectively, the home marginal propensities to spend on imports and on nontraded goods, and let m^* and n^* denote the analogous foreign parameters. Then, at the initial prices for all goods, the resulting excess demands on each market are:

home imports: $(1 - m - m^* - n^*)T$
home exports: $- (1 - m - m^* - n)T$
home nontraded goods: $-nT$
foreign nontraded goods: n^*T.

If any of these terms differ from zero, prices will change in response to the transfer. If $n = n^* = 0$, the earlier analysis continues to hold. Otherwise the situation is more complex. There will be an excess demand for home imports and excess supply of home exports if $1 - m - m^*$ exceeds both n and n^*, whereas before it had to exceed only 0 for the same situation to obtain. Also, the resulting price changes will have to be such as to restore equilibrium in both nontraded goods markets, as well as in the markets for traded goods.

Additional Problems

1. Suppose that Samos makes a transfer of 1,000 drachmas to Chios. Samos has a marginal propensity to import of 1/2 and Chios a marginal propensity to spend on exportables of 1/4. Describe as fully as possible the effects of this transfer.

2. The discussion in the text assumed just two countries, the payer and the receiver. Suppose that there is a third country, the rest of the world, which does not participate in the transfer payment but with

which both the paying and the receiving countries trade. How are our conclusions affected?

Answers to Self-Test

1. False.

2. 2.3.

6. Direct Investment and the Multinational Corporation

Basic Ideas

1. About one-fourth of world trade actually takes place within multi-national corporations.

2. Most of the largest MNEs are U.S. based, and the United States is both a heavy net creditor with regard to direct investment and the source of a large part of world direct investment. However foreign MNEs and foreign direct investment in the United States are growing rapidly.

3. The larger share of world direct investment takes place between those parts of the globe (DCs) that also trade the most with each other.

4. Any theory of the MNE must explain why a certain market is serviced by the subsidiary of a foreign corporation rather than by independent domestic firms, by domestic firms under license to the foreign corp-oration, or by imports from the foreign corporation.

5. The predominant explanation for the existence of MNEs consists of three parts.

   a. The firm possesses some unique attribute that can be exploited for profit in a foreign market.

   b. Because of comparative cost considerations it is advantageous to exploit this attribute by means of foreign production.

   c. It is cheaper to internalize the transfer of the attribute than to transfer it through markets.

6. Terms you should understand: **vertical integration, horizontal integration, internalization of transactions, joint venture.**

Self-Test

1. True or false: Direct investment is much more important in the world economy now than it was before the Second World War.

2. True or false: Because of technological advances in communications and other areas, direct investment is a much larger share of total U.S. foreign investment than it was earlier in the century.

3. Multiple choice: Which of the following statements is not true?
3.1. About one-quarter of world trade is intrafirm.
3.2. Most direct investment comes from the DCs, and nearly half of it has come from the United States.
3.3. Nearly three-quarters of world direct investment has been directed towards the DCs.
3.4. All of the above.
3.5. None of the above.

4. True or false: Direct investments by U.S. firms in Europe constitute movements of capital from the United States to Europe.

Solutions to Problems from the Text

6.20 *Give an example of a vertically integrated MNE in a natural-resource industry. Why is it "natural" for firms in such industries to integrate vertically? Can you explain this in terms of our general theory of why firms go multinational?*

Consider large oil firms.

6.22 *IBM decided to close down its operations in India rather than to comply with a law requiring substantial local ownership. Can you think of any reasons why IBM would prefer doing no business at all to participating in a joint venture?*

A joint venture could easily have resulted in disclosing technical secrets to the partners in the venture. Also, IBM may have wished to demonstrate to other countries contemplating similar local ownership requirements that it would in fact pull out entirely in response.

Additional Problems

1. Try to reconcile the observation that the larger part of direct investment is within the group of countries that trade the most with each other, and the argument of section 1 of the textbook that trade and factor movements are substitutes.

2. Pick one MNE from Table 6.8 in the textbook and research its global operations in detail. Try to interpret what you uncover in terms of the theory of this section of the text.

3. Suppose that you are an executive in a firm with a valuable patent to be exploited in a foreign market. You must choose whether to do so by setting up a foreign subsidiary or by licensing the patent to a foreign firm. What concrete factors would you consider?

1. True.

2. False.

3. 3.4.

4. False.

7. Public Policy toward the Multinational Enterprise

Basic Ideas

1. Because political integration has not proceeded in step with the economic integration embodied in MNEs, the latter pose problems for national governments.

2. MNEs can erode the ability of national governments to conduct policy, can help generate conflict between governments, and can become the vehicles for already existing international conflict.

3. Source countries have problems regarding the taxation of MNEs, and labor in these countries often sees the MNE as an exporter of jobs.

4. Host countries sometimes feel exploited by MNEs and often complain that the latter do not bring in enough capital and new technology.

Self-Test

1. What are transfer prices?

2. Multiple choice: Which of the following is true?
   2.1. U.S. MNEs pay no taxes on foreign earnings.
   2.2. The foreign tax bill of U.S. MNEs is reduced by the amount of any U.S. taxes that they pay.
   2.3. MNEs must pay taxes on foreign earnings when those earnings are repatriated.
   2.4. All of the above.
   2.5. None of the above.

3. Multiple choice: Which of the following countries has not screened foreign direct investment projects before allowing them to take place?
   3.1. France.
   3.2. Germany.
   3.3. Japan.
   3.4. Canada.
   3.5. None of the above.

4. True or false: Labor generally supports inward direct investment and opposes outward direct investment.

Answers to Self-Test

1. Prices that one part of an MNE charges to another part.

2. 2.3.

3. 3.2.

4. True.

8. Review Questions

1. In what ways is the international exchange of factors similar to the international trade of goods? In what ways is it different?

2. In what ways is the international movement of labor similar to the international movement of capital? In what ways is it different?

3. Discuss whether international factor mobility and international trade are likely to be substitutes or complements.

PART THREE

International Monetary Theory and Its Application

CHAPTER 7   The Exchange Rate

1. Balance of Payments Accounts

Basic Ideas

1. A country's balance of payments accounts are a record of transactions in a specific time interval between residents of that country and the rest of the world.

2. Each transaction generates two equal entries in the accounts, a credit (+) for an export of a good, service, or asset, or for the receipt of a unilateral transfer, and a debit (−) for an import of a good, service, or asset, or for making a unilateral transfer.

3. Be sure you know: **how to tell a credit from a debit, what the various detailed subaccounts refer to.**

Solutions to Problems from the Text

7.1 *A U.K. distillery sells an American firm 200 cases of whiskey in exchange for a $25,000 check drawn on an American bank. The distillery uses $15,000 of this to buy equipment in France, and the other $10,000 to retire bonds it had issued years ago to a group of wealthy Italian investors. Write all the resulting entries in the balance of payments accounts of the United States, France, the United Kingdom, Germany, and Italy.*

U.S.: $25,000 debit, merchandise imports; $25,000 credit, short-term capital. France: $15,000 credit, merchandise exports; $15,000 debit, short-term capital. U.K.: $25,000 credit, merchandise exports; $25,000 debit, short-term capital; $15,000 debit, merchandise imports; $15,000 credit, short-term capital; $10,000 debit, long-term capital; $10,000 credit, short-term capital. Germany: no entries. Italy: $10,000 credit, long-term capital; $10,000 debit, short-term capital.

7.2 *Write all balance of payments entries resulting from each of the following transactions.*

a. *The U.S. Army gives $1 million in pay to American soldiers stationed in Germany.*

b. *Ford Motor Company (U.S.) pays $1 million to Ford's German subsidiary for automobile parts.*

c. *An American automobile dealer pays $1 million, by check, to the German firm BMW for automobiles.*

d. BMW pays $1 million to the Bundesbank for DM1.6 million.

e. Daring Danny of Denver, sky-diving champion of all Colorado west of the Rockies, pays Lloyds of London $10,000 for a life insurance policy.

f. Lloyds of London pays Daring Danny's widow $1 million in settlement of a life-insurance policy claim.

g. A Japanese firm sends the Soviet Union $2 million worth of drilling equipment in return for $2 million worth of oil.

h. A Japanese firm sends the Soviet Union $2 million worth of drilling equipment in return for a promise of $4 million worth of oil in five years.

i. You visit Singapore and have $1,000 stolen by a local pickpocket.

j. You visit Singapore and lose $1,000 worth of American traveler's checks, for which you receive a refund from the local bank.

a. No entries.

b. U.S.: $1 million debit for merchandise imports; $1 million credit, short-term capital. The reverse for Germany.

c. Same as part b.

d. U.S.: $1 million debit, short-term capital; $1 million credit, liabilities to foreign official institutions. The reverse for Germany.

e. U.S.: $10,000 debit, $10,000 credit, short-term capital. The reverse for the U.K.

f. U.S.: $1 million credit, transfers; $1 million debit, short-term capital. The reverse for the U.K.

g. Japan: $2 million credit, merchandise exports; $2 million debit, merchandise imports. The same for the Soviet Union.

h. Japan: $2 million credit, merchandise exports; $2 million debit, long-term capital. The reverse for the Soviet Union.

i. U.S. (or whatever country you're a resident of): $1,000 credit, short-term capital; $1,000 debit, transfers. The reverse for Singapore.

j. U.S.: $1,000 credit, short-term capital; $1,000 debit, short-term capital.

7.3 *Generally, only transactions between American residents and foreign residents generate entries in the American balance of payments. But in one case, transactions between two foreigners result in such entries. What is this case?*

When foreign residents sell U.S. dollar assets to a foreign central bank.

*7.4 Consider Canada's balance of payments, as described in the table below.

    a. Discuss each line, as the text did for Table 7.1. In what ways do Canada's payments differ from those of the United States? Why?

    b. What is the item "Change in Value of Reserves"? To what is a negative number due?

CANADIAN BALANCE OF PAYMENTS, 1985 (*billions of Canadian dollars*)

Merchandise Trade	17.3	
Services	−21.0	
[*Goods and Services*		−3.7]
Private Unilateral Transfers	1.2	
Official Unilateral Transfers	−.2	
Total Current Account		−2.7
Direct Investment	−7.3	
Portfolio Investment	9.7	
Other Nonofficial Capital	3.2	
Total Nonofficial Capital		5.6
Net Errors and Omissions	−3.3	−3.3
Change in Value of Reserves	−.3	
Official Reserve Assets	.7	
Net Official Reserve Transactions		.4
	0.0	

SOURCE: IMF, *Balance of Payments Statistics.*

A significant part of Canadian international reserves consists of assets denominated in U.S. dollars. If the exchange rate of the latter in terms of Canadian dollars changes, the value of these assets in terms of Canadian dollars likewise changes. This accounts for the item "Change in Value of Reserves." The negative entry in the table could be produced by an appreciation of the Canadian dollar relative to the U.S. dollar.

Additional Problems

1. Look up the most recent detailed presentation of U.S. balance of payments statistics (see Appendix II of the textbook for data sources). Be sure you can explain the meaning of each entry. Reorganize the data in the same form as Table 7.1 in the textbook. Compare with Table 7.1.

2. Look up the most recent detailed presentation of Canadian balance of payments statistics (see Appendix II of the textbook for data sources).

Be sure you can explain the meaning of each entry. Reorganize the data in the same form as the table in Problem *7.4 above. Compare with that table.

2. International Monetary Equilibrium

Basic Ideas

1. This chapter examines the operation of an international monetary system when exchange rates may vary.

2. Assuming the quantity theory of money, the equilibrium terms of trade determines the equilibrium relative values of various countries' money supplies.

3. The actual absolute sizes of various countries' money supplies then determine the equilibrium value of the exchange rate.

Self-Test

1. True or false: According to the theory of this section, the money supplies of two trading countries will have no effect at all upon their equilibrium terms of trade.

2. Multiple choice: At unchanged terms of trade, an increase in the German money supply will:
   2.1. Increase the French equilibrium exchange rate.
   2.2. Increase the German equilibrium exchange rate.
   2.3. Increase the French money supply.
   2.4. Lower the German equilibrium exchange rate.
   2.5. None of the above.

3. Multiple choice: If real outputs remain unchanged in France and Germany, a deterioration of the German terms of trade will:
   3.1. Increase the French equilibrium exchange rate.
   3.2. Increase the German equilibrium exchange rate.
   3.3. Increase the French money supply.
   3.4. Lower the French equilibrium exchange rate.
   3.5. None of the above.

Solutions to Problems from the Text

7.5 *Suppose that whiskey costs £120 per case, that wheat costs $90 per bushel, and that the relative price of whiskey in terms of wheat is two bushels per case. What is the U.S. exchange rate, the price of a pound in terms of dollars? What is the dollar price of whiskey? The pound price of wheat?*

The U.S. exchange rate is $1.50/£, the price of whiskey is $180, and the price of wheat is £60.

7.6 *Suppose that the United States and Europe trade, the United States specializing in and exporting wheat and Europe special-*

*izing in and exporting cloth. U.S. wheat production equals 1,000
and European cloth production 600. In equilibrium 5 wheat exchange for 1 cloth. The U.S. money supply consists of $2,000,
the European money supply consists of £3,000, and k equals 1/2.
Describe international monetary equilibrium and illustrate with
a diagram analogous to Figure 7.1 in the textbook. Suppose the
U.S. money supply increases to $4,000; calculate the effect on
your answer and illustrate the change in your diagram. Do the
same if instead the terms of trade were to alter so that 5 wheat
exchange for 3 cloth.*

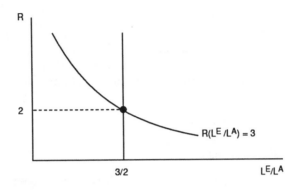

The American exchange rate $R = \$2/£$. If $L^A = \$4,000$, then $R = \$4/£$.
If $R(P_C/P_W) = 5/3$, then $R = \$.67/£$.

7.7 *In the discussion in the text, how will the French equilibrium
exchange rate be affected by:*

    a. *An improvement in the French terms of trade; or*

    b. *A growth of German income relative to French?*

An improvement in the terms of trade (a fall in p) causes the franc to
appreciate (a fall in R); a relative growth of German income causes
the franc to depreciate.

7.8 *Suppose that the franc becomes worth fewer marks (so R
rises). What will be the direct impact of this on French and
German firms if they pursue the following alternative pricing
policies:*

    a. *Each firm holds the domestic currency price of its product
fixed and adjusts the foreign currency price;*

    b. *Each firm holds constant in foreign currency the price of its
product and adjusts the domestic currency price; or*

    c. *Each firm holds constant both the domestic currency price at
which it sells in domestic markets and also the foreign
currency price at which it sells in foreign markets.*

What consequences would likely develop in each case for the respective firms? Can you think of any reason why firms might respond in one way rather than in others?

Case a: French firms lower the mark price of their exports and German firms raise the franc price of their exports, so that French goods become cheaper relative to German goods in both markets.

Case b: French firms raise their domestic prices and German firms lower their domestic prices, so that French goods become more expensive relative to German in both markets.

Case c: French firms receive a higher price for exports than for domestic sales, while German firms receive a lower price for exports than for domestic sales.

7.9 *Show the effects of an increase in the French money supply in Figure 7.1 in the textbook. What happens to the equilibrium exchange rate if the French increase their money supply by 25 percent each and every year? What happens to the money prices of both goods?*

The SS' line shifts to the left, causing R to rise.

Additional Problems

1. Draw Figure 7.1 in the textbook as it would appear if France were a very small country relative to Germany. (Imagine Germany to be the rest of the world.)

2. Suppose that Gormengast and Ditch trade, Gormengast specializing in and exporting zingoes and Ditch specializing in and exporting poobahs. Gormengast's zingo production equals 10,000 and Ditch's poobah production 20. In equilibrium 100 zingoes exchange for 1 poobah. The Gormengastian money supply consists of 12,000 clams, Ditch's money supply is 12,000 oysters, and k equals 2. Describe international monetary equilibrium and illustrate with a diagram analogous to Figure 7.1 in the textbook. Suppose the Gormengastian money supply increases to 18,000 clams; calculate the effect on your answer and illustrate the change in your diagram. Do the same if instead the terms of trade were to alter so that 150 zingoes exchange for 3 poobahs.

3. The discussion in the textbook supposed that k had the same value in both countries. Show in detail how the argument would change if k were different in Germany and France. How would your answer to the first part of Problem 7.6 above change if k were to fall to 1/4 in America but remain at 1/2 in Europe?

Answers to Self-Test

1. True.

2. 2.2.

3. 3.4.

3. Exchange-Rate Adjustment

Basic Ideas

1. If the actual exchange rate does not equal the equilibrium exchange rate, as described in the previous section, adjustment is necessary.

2. This adjustment can take any of three alternative forms:

   a. Through payments imbalances, which change the relative money supplies of the two countries.

   b. Through exchange-rate variations.

   c. Through a combination of payments imbalances and exchange-rate variations.

3. If adjustment takes place through exchange-rate variations, there are two broad implications:

   a. Individual countries can control their own money supplies.

   b. Payments imbalances can be controlled or prevented by exchange-rate adjustment.

4. Terms to know: **appreciation and depreciation; revaluation and devaluation.**

Self-Test

1. Suppose the dollar depreciates relative to all other currencies. For each of the following, write a "W" if, other things constant, the depreciation is likely to be welcomed by the person described, and a "D" if the depreciation is likely to be disliked.
   1.1. Someone with wealth in dollars.
   1.2. Someone with wealth in British pounds.
   1.3. Someone selling goods priced in dollars.
   1.4. Someone selling goods priced in British pounds.
   1.5. Someone importing goods priced in dollars.

2. Distinguish between "depreciation" and "devaluation."

3. Multiple choice: Which of the following pairs represents two alternative methods of adjustment:
   3.1. Appreciation or payments deficits.
   3.2. Depreciation or payments surpluses.
   3.3. Depreciation or revaluation.
   3.4. All of the above.
   3.5. None of the above.

Solutions to Problems from the Text

7.10 *As in Problem 7.6, America produces 1,000 wheat, Europe 600 cloth, and in equilibrium 5 wheat exchange for 1 cloth. Initially, the U.S. money supply consists of $2,000, the European money supply is £3,000 and k = 1/2. Now suppose that the U.S. money* *supply increases to $4,000. Calculate the cumulative payments imbalance necessary to restore equilibrium if the exchange rate were held fixed. What exchange-rate adjustment would instead be required if the U.S. money supply were maintained at $4,000? What would happen if, after the initial increase in the U.S. money supply to $4,000, the authorities decided not to let it subsequently fall below $3,000?*

A cumulative U.S. deficit of $1,500, or a depreciation of the dollar to $4 per pound, or a cumulative U.S. deficit of $1,000 followed by a depreciation of the dollar to $2.57 per pound would each suffice to restore equilibrium.

7.11 *Suppose that England is on a gold standard, China on a silver standard, and France on a bimetallic standard. France increases the franc price of silver but does not change the price of gold. Which currencies have devalued, revalued, depreciated, or appreciated, and relative to what?*

France devalues relative to silver but not to gold; France depreciates relative to China but not to England; China appreciates relative to France but not to England. Neither China nor England devalue or revalue.

7.12 *Suppose that German real income y^G grows by 10 percent each year, but that French real income y^F remains constant. What happens to international equilibrium if the French increase the supply of francs by 5 percent a year and Germany increases the supply of marks by 10 percent per year?*

R rises (that is, the franc depreciates) by 5 percent per year.

7.13 *In the last two columns of the table,* Selected Exchange Rates, *in the introduction to Part Three of the textbook, which currencies are shown to have appreciated and which to have depreciated relative to the U.S. dollar? Relative to the franc?*

The Canadian dollar and the peso depreciated, and the yen, franc, mark, and pound appreciated relative to the U.S. dollar. The franc depreciated relative to the mark and appreciated relative to all other currencies in the table.

Additional Problem

1. In Problem 7.10, suppose that the American money supply remains equal to $2,000, but that economic growth in America raises wheat production to 2,000 units. Calculate the cumulative payments imbalance necessary to restore equilibrium. What exchange-rate adjustment would do so instead?

Answers to Self-Test

1. 1.1. D.
   1.2. W.

1.3. W.
1.4. D.
1.5. W.

2. 2.5.

4. Exchange Regimes in Practice

Basic Ideas

1. This section examines present day exchange-rate arrangements. The most notable characteristic of these arrangements is their diversity.

2. The major industrial nations have managed floats with respect to each other. The notable exception is the adjustable peg arrangement among the nations participating in the European Monetary System.

3. Most LDCs maintain an adjustable peg to the dollar or to a basket of currencies, or, in some cases, to some single currency other than the dollar.

4. Extensive exchange controls are also common among LDCs.

5. Individual countries apply these regimes in quite different ways, and any single country is apt to significantly alter its practices over time.

6. The basic advantage of fixed exchange rates is that they make a country's currency more useful as money.

7. The basic advantage of flexible rates is that they allow a country to control its own money supply.

Self-Test

1. What does EMS stand for?

2. What is a dual exchange market?

3. Multiple choice: Most LDCs:
   3.1. Have floating exchange rates because they cannot afford the reserves necessary to peg.
   3.2. Cannot practice exchange control because of a lack of trained bureaucrats.
   3.3. Encourage capital mobility.
   3.4. Remain on the gold standard.
   3.5. None of the above.

Solutions to Problems from the Text

7.17 *This section of the textbook gave reasons why a country might wish to peg its currency rather than to float. But why might it want to peg to a currency basket rather than to some individual currency? What considerations might influence the decision of which currency basket to peg to? Does it matter whether the authorities hold a commodity flow or an asset market view of the exchange rate?*

A country might hope to stabilize its terms of trade by pegging its exchange rate; if this is the motive, it is natural to peg to a basket reflecting the relative importance of the various currencies of denomination of that country's imports and exports. Alternatively, a country might peg in order to maximize the value of that country's currency as money, and thereby encourage people to hold that currency and also encourage the development of domestic financial facilities. In this case the most natural basket would be one reflecting people's pattern of purchases. The first motive is more consistent with a commodity flow view of the exchange rate, the second more consistent with an asset market view.

7.18 *With a pegged exchange rate the authorities usually establish a band around the peg within which the exchange rate is allowed to float, perhaps freely, perhaps not. Under the gold standard a similar band was common, not because of policy, but because of the cost (shipping, insurance, and foregone interest) of transporting gold from one country to another. Suppose that in Paris the French authorities freely exchanged gold and francs at the rate of fr100/ounce, while in Berlin the German authorities bought and sold gold for DM50/ounce. Suppose it cost the equivalent of one-tenth of an ounce of gold to transport each ounce between Paris and Berlin. Calculate the band within which the franc price of a mark must fall.*

Between fr1.8 and fr2.22 per DM.

Additional Problems

1. Investigate which countries of the world peg their currencies and which float (see Appendix II of the textbook for data sources). Pick three examples of each and try to explain why they are doing what they are doing.

2. Do more countries peg than float, or is the reverse the case? Is more of world trade between countries whose currencies are pegged to each other, or between countries whose currencies float relative to each other?

Answers to Self-Test

1. European Monetary System.

2. One in which current-account transactions are segregated from capital-account transactions, so that they are subject to different exchange rates. Often the current-account rate is pegged while the capital-account rate is not.

3. 3.5.

5. International Capital Mobility

Basic Ideas

1. This section examines the effect of depreciation upon the capital account.

2. Individuals must decide how to divide their wealth between money and bonds, and also between assets denominated in domestic currency and those denominated in foreign currency.

3. Both the *level* of the exchange rate and its *expected change* influence individuals' portfolio choices.

4. The level of the exchange rate matters because it determines how many foreign-currency denominated assets a given amount of domestic currency will buy, and how many domestic-currency assets a given amount of foreign currency will buy.

5. The expected change in the exchange rate matters because it is part of the expected yield of holding assets denominated in terms of foreign currency.

6. The degree of international capital mobility determines how closely linked together are interest rates of assets denominated in different currencies.

7. With perfect international capital mobility, interest parity will hold: the excess of domestic interest rates over foreign interest rates will exactly reflect the expected rate of depreciation of the domestic currency.

8. It is very difficult to tell how closely interest parity actually holds because we cannot observe expected rates of depreciation.

Self-Test

1. True or false: With imperfect capital mobility, an expected appreciation of the exchange rate will reduce interest rates at home, relative to those abroad, but not by as much as it would if there were no capital mobility at all.

Solutions to Problems from the Text

7.19 *If the U.S. rate of interest is 6 percent and the comparable U.K. interest rate is 9 percent, what must the consensus view be about the likely future course of the dollar-sterling exchange rate, if interest parity is to hold?*

That the pound is expected to depreciate by 3 percent relative to the dollar.

7.20 *The formula for interest parity given in the text applies instan-taneously for assets that are about to mature. The formula varies*

slightly for different maturities. Suppose, for example, that r
denotes what a dollar invested in the United States will earn in
interest over the next three months, that r* *is the number of*
pounds sterling a pound invested in the United Kingdom would
earn over the next three, that R *is the current U.S. exchange*
rate (the number of dollars required to buy one pound now),
and that E *denotes what this exchange rate is expected to be in*
three months. Then interest parity will hold if (1 + r) =
(1/R)(1 + r*)E. Explain why. The formula can also be written:

$$\frac{E - R}{R} = r - \frac{E}{R} r^*.$$

Derive this expression. The term on the left is the expected
depreciation of the dollar relative to the pound over the next
three months. Newspapers will quote three-month interest rates
on an annualized basis. To obtain r from such a quote, divide the
latter by 4 (to change it from an annual basis to a three-month
basis), and then divide by 100 (to change it from a percentage
to a decimal). Thus a three-month interest rate of 12 percent
corresponds to a value of r of .03. (The above formula converges
to the one in the text as the time to maturity becomes
arbitrarily small.)

If a dollar is invested in the United States, it will be worth $1 + r$
dollars in three months. If it is instead invested in the United Kingdom, the dollar will buy $(1/R)$ pounds now, each pound invested in
the United Kingdom will be worth $1 + r^*$ pounds in three months,
and it is expected that in three months each pound will be sold for E
dollars. Thus a dollar invested in the United Kingdom now is expected
to be worth $(1/R)(1 + r^*)E$ dollars in three months. Interest parity
implies that a dollar invested now in the United States is expected to
be worth the same number of dollars in three months as a dollar invested in the United Kingdom: $1 + r = (1/R)(1 + r^*)E$. Subtract
$1 - (E/R)r^*$ from both sides to obtain the other version of this
formula.

7.21 *Suppose that the present exchange rate is $1.50/£ and that in*
the U.S. the three-month, six-month, and one-year interest
rates are respectively 12 percent, 10 percent, and 8 percent, on
a yearly basis. The corresponding U.K. interest rates are 6
percent, 10 percent, and 10 percent. Describe what the market
must expect the future course of the exchange rate to be, if
interest parity holds.

The dollar is expected to depreciate to $1.5225/£ in three months, to
then appreciate back to $1.50/£ in six months, and to appreciate
further to $1.47/£ in one year.

Additional Problems

1. Use Figure 7.5 in the textbook to depict the effect of a depreciation of
   the franc that is expected to be temporary.

2. Use Figure 7.5 in the textbook to depict the effect of a depreciation of the franc that is expected to be permanent.

3. Use Figure 7.5 in the textbook to depict the effect of a depreciation of the franc that is expected to be just the first step in a prolonged process of depreciation.

Answer to Self-Test

1. True.

6. Portfolio Balance and the Exchange Rate

Basic Ideas

1. Portfolio balance requires simultaneous equilibrium in money and bond markets.

2. The exchange rate and both interest rates must be such that:

   a. The exchange rate clears the money markets, given interest rates, and

   b. Interest rates clear the bond markets, given the exchange rate.

3. The exchange rate has a dual role to play, as discussed in the previous section. The *level* of the exchange rate matters because it influences the relative *values* of assets denominated in different currencies, and the *expected change* in the exchange rate also matters because it affects the *return* to assets denominated in one currency relative to the return to assets denominated in another currency.

Self-Test

1. What will be the direct effect on the exchange rate of a fall in the home rate of interest?

2. What will be the direct effect on the home rate of interest of a depreciation of the domestic currency?

Solutions to Problems from the Text

7.22 *Suppose that some exogenous shock to the world economy causes the DD' curve in Figure 7.6 in the textbook to shift upwards. Give an example of a shock that could do this. Analyze the implications for equilibrium.*

DD' would be shifted up by any disturbance that caused equilibrium prices in Germany to rise relative to those in France, such as a change in preferences toward German goods and away from French goods. Another possible cause would be any disturbance that raised k in Germany relative to that in France, such as an improvement in the French payments mechanism due to the introduction of credit cards. The resulting depreciation of the franc shifts FF down and GG to the left.

7.23 *Suppose that the depreciation of the franc that occurred in your answer to Problem 7.22 is regarded by the market as temporary. That is, people expect that in the future it will appreciate back to where it was originally. How does this change your answer to Problem 7.22?*

Since people come to expect an appreciation of the franc, d falls so that IP shifts down and a downward shift of FF and a rightward shift of GG are added to the disturbances in Problem 7.22.

7.24 *What will Figure 7.6 in the textbook look like if capital mobility is perfect? Analyze the effects of a change in d in this case.*

The FF and GG lines collapse to a single point on the IP line.

7.25 *Write the German analog to equation (7.5) in the textbook.*

$$B^* = \frac{[1 - b(i_f, i_g + d)][W^F - L^F]}{R} + b^*(i_f - d, i_g)[W^G - L^G],$$

where B^* denotes the total supply of mark denominated bonds.

7.26 *What would have happened, in Problem 7.23, if people had regarded the depreciation of the franc as temporary, but as merely the first in a series of depreciations, rather than as a change to be reversed?*

Now people come to expect a further depreciation of the franc, so d rises and IP shifts up. An upward shift of FF and a leftward shift of GG are added to the disturbances in Problem 7.22.

Answers to Self-Test

1. It will appreciate.
2. It will fall.

7. Monetary Policy and Exchange Rates

Basic Ideas

1. This section puts the portfolio balance model to work to analyze the effects of monetary policy and intervention in the foreign exchange markets.

2. An open-market purchase of bonds reduces total demand by domestic residents for home and foreign bonds by the same amount that it reduces the supply of home bonds. This reduces interest rates at home

and raises them abroad. The changes in interest rates cause shifts in the demands for home and foreign money, producing a depreciation.

3. Intervention alters the relative supplies of home and foreign monies thereby influencing the exchange rate. Variations in the latter affect the bond markets, causing interest rates to change.

Self-Test

1. Show how a central bank's balance sheet is affected by an expansionary open market operation of ΔM.

2. Show how a central bank's balance sheet is affected by unsterilized intervention of ΔU in support of the domestic currency.

3. Show how a central bank's balance sheet is affected by sterilized intervention of ΔS in support of the domestic currency.

Solutions to Problems from the Text

7.27 *Analyze the effect of an increase in French wealth on international portfolio equilibrium.*

The exact effect depends upon the form that the increase in wealth takes. If it consists entirely of an increase in the stock of French bonds, *FF* shifts up and *GG* shifts to the left.

7.28 *The text analyzed the effect of intervention to support the mark on the assumption that expectations* d *about the future course of the exchange rate are unaffected by the intervention. Suppose instead that the public believes that this intervention will have only a temporary effect, that is, that they revise* d *to reflect a belief that the mark will depreciate back in the future. How does this affect our analysis of devaluation?*

In this case the intervention is accompanied by a *fall* in d since the franc is now expected to appreciate. Thus the effects associated with a fall in d must be superimposed on those discussed in the text.

7.29 *How does your answer to Problem 7.28 change if the public instead interprets the intervention in support of the mark as just the opening shot in a long campaign, that is, if they expect the mark to appreciate even more?*

Now d rises instead, so just the opposite effects are superimposed.

*7.30 *Intervention to support a currency reduces the supply of that currency, and intervention to induce depreciation increases the supply. But in practice intervention is often sterilized by offsetting open market operations. That is, a central bank supporting its currency by selling international reserves for money will at the same time buy bonds with money. The net result is that the money supply remains fixed, with the central bank exchang-*

ing international reserves for bonds. How is our analysis of intervention changed if the French central bank sterilizes its intervention? If both central banks sterilize?

Your analysis should remain much the same qualitatively, but now the direct effects will be in the bond markets, with indirect effects in all markets.

Answers to Self-Test

1.

ASSETS	LIABILITIES
Government Bonds: $+\Delta M$	Commercial Bank Reserves: $+\Delta M$
International Reserves: 0	

2.

ASSETS	LIABILITIES
Government Bonds: 0	Commercial Bank Reserves: $-\Delta U$
International Reserves: $-\Delta U$	

3.

ASSETS	LIABILITIES
Government Bonds: $+\Delta S$	Commercial Bank Reserves: 0
International Reserves: $-\Delta S$	

*8. Exploring Further: An Intertemporal View of Capital Movements

Basic Ideas

1. Two-commodity trade models can be used to study the current account (capital account) from an intertemporal perspective if the goods are thought of as "present goods" and "future goods."

2. The relative price of present goods in terms of future goods is one plus the rate of interest.

3. A net import of present goods in exchange for future goods constitutes a present current-account deficit (or capital-account surplus).

4. Since the demand for money in a country depends upon the quantity of goods currently being consumed in that country, the intertemporal view of the current account also offers an explanation for the behavior of the exchange rate over time.

Solutions to Problems from the Text

7.31 *Suppose that France and Germany move from autarky to the situation shown in Figures 7.10 and 7.11 in the text. Describe in detail the effects on firms and consumers in both countries, and the effects on money market equilibrium.*

Initially the interest rate in France is *OF* minus one, in Figure 7.10 in the text. When free international transactions are allowed, French residents find themselves exposed to a lower interest rate. This induces French consumers to save less (and spend more now) and French firms to invest more. The opposite takes place in Germany. The increased present consumption of goods in France and the reduced present consumption in Germany raise the demand for francs relative to the demand for marks, and the franc appreciates.

7.32 *The discussion in the text assumed perfect capital mobility: a single world rate of interest was established. Suppose instead that in the present everyone believes that the German government will in the future impose a tax on interest income received from abroad. How does this affect international equilibrium?*

The German excess supply curve shifts up by the amount of the tax. The intersection of the French curve with the new German curve determines the interest rate in France, and the interest rate in Germany is lower by the amount of the tax.

*7.33 *In this section perfect capital mobility was taken to imply a single world rate of interest. But the theory also allows the exchange rate to vary from the present to the future, so people are likely to have expectations about these variations. Earlier in this chapter we saw that perfect capital mobility was characterized by uncovered interest parity: interest rates differ by expected changes in the exchange rate. Is the present section inconsistent with this?*

The single world interest rate determined by the theory in this section of the text is the *real* rate of interest. *Nominal* interest rates in the two countries would differ by the expected future change in the exchange rate as called for by uncovered interest parity.

*7.34 *The equilibrium depicted in Figures 7.10 and 7.11 calls for the franc to depreciate in the future. But if people realize that this* *is going to happen, they will want to take care that, when the future arrives, they are holding few francs and many marks. How would this consideration affect the analysis in the text?*

People would be less willing, now, to hold francs and more willing to hold marks. Thus today's *DD'* curve will shift up because of expectations about how the exchange rate will behave in the future. This shift causes the franc to depreciate now.

Additional Problems

1. What happens to the equilibrium in Figures 7.10 and 7.11 in the text if France imposes a tariff on the import of German goods, and spends the proceeds on future goods?

2. What happens to the equilibrium in Figures 7.10 and 7.11 in the text if German lenders begin to fear that there is a chance that French borrowers will default on their loans when the future arrives?

9. Review Questions

1. Discuss the implications of exchange rate adjustment.

2. Discuss alternative methods of international adjustment.

3. What are the implications of the degree of international capital mobility for exchange rate adjustment?

CHAPTER 8   The Automatic Adjustment Process

1. International Monetary Equilibrium

Basic Ideas

1. This chapter examines the operation of an international monetary system characterized by fixed exchange rates. With fixed rates it is meaningful to add together the money supplies of different countries to obtain the size of the world money supply.

2. Assuming the quantity theory of money, the equilibrium terms of trade determines the equilibrium relative sizes of various countries' money supplies.

3. The size of the world money supply then determines the equilibrium absolute sizes of various countries' money supplies and absolute price levels.

Self-Test

1. Multiple choice: The crude quantity theory of money implies that:
    1.1. The price level is proportional to the money supply.
    1.2. Real output is proportional to the money supply.
    1.3. The price level is proportional to real output.
    1.4. All of the above.
    1.5. None of the above.

2. True or false: According to the theory of this section, the money supplies of two trading countries will have no effect at all upon their equilibrium terms of trade.

Solutions to Problems from the Text

8.1 *Suppose that America and Europe trade, America specializing in and exporting wheat and Europe specializing in and exporting cloth. American wheat production equals 1,000 and European cloth production 600. In equilibrium 5 wheat exchange for 1 cloth. The world money supply consists of 2,000 gold coins, and k equals 1/2. Describe international monetary equilibrium and illustrate with a diagram analogous to Figure 8.1 in the textbook. Suppose the world money supply increases to 4,000 gold* coins; calculate the effect on your answer and illustrate the change in your diagram. Do the same if instead the terms of trade were to alter so that 5 wheat exchange for 3 cloth.

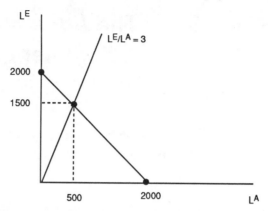

Thus, $L^A = 500$, $L^E = 1,500$, $P_W = 1$, $P_C = 5$. If $L^A + L^E = 4,000$, then $L^A = 1,000$, $L^E = 3,000$, $P_W = 2$ and $P_C = 10$. If $P_W/P_C = 3/5$, $L^A = 1,000 = L^E$.

8.2 *The discussion in the textbook supposed that k had the same value in both countries. Show in detail how the argument would change if k were different in Germany than in France. How would your answer to the first part of the above problem change if k were to fall to 1/4 in America but remain at 1/2 in Europe?*

If k differed in the two countries, then equation (8.3) in the text would become: $L^G/L^F = p(y^G/y^F)(k^G/k^F)$. If k were to fall to 1/4 in America, in Problem 8.1, then the American money supply would equal 285.7 and the European money supply would equal 1,714.3 in equilibrium.

8.3 *Assume that in equilibrium the German supply of butane is 111 and supply of apples is 21, that France exports 70 apples to Germany for 30 units of butane, and that French production is 100 apples. Suppose that the world money supply consists of 1,520 gold coins and that k equals 2. Find the equilibrium money supplies in the two countries and the equilibrium money prices of the two goods.*

The German money supply is 1,120, the French money supply is 400, the price of butane is 4.67, and the price of an apple is 2.

*8.4 *England has 100 labor units, of which 5 are required to produce either a cask of wine or a bolt of cloth. The English always consume equal quantities of the two goods. Portugal has 100 labor units with 1 required to produce a cask of wine and 4 to produce a bolt of cloth; the Portuguese always consume equal valued quantities of wine and cloth. The world money supply consists of 150 gold coins, and k equals 1. Describe and illustrate international monetary equilibrium. Show what happens if England's labor force increases to 1,000.*

In equilibrium the English money supply is 66.67 gold coins and the Portuguese is 83.33; the price of cloth is 3.33 coins and the price of wine is .83. If the English labor force increases to 1,000, then in the new equilibrium the English money supply is 100 gold coins and the Portuguese is 50; the prices of wine and cloth each equal 1/2 of a gold coin.

*8.5 Show how the discussion in this section of the textbook changes if, instead of remaining fixed, L constantly increases at the rate of 10 percent per year.

The two money supplies and the two nominal prices all increase at 10 percent per year. All other magnitudes are unchanged.

Additional Problems

1. Draw Figure 8.1 in the textbook as it would appear if France were a very small country relative to Germany. (Imagine Germany to be the rest of the world.)

2. Suppose that Gormengast and Ditch trade, Gormengast specializing in and exporting zingoes and Ditch specializing in and exporting poobahs. Gormengast's zingo production equals 10,000 and Ditch's poobah production 20. In equilibrium 100 zingoes exchange for 1 poobah. The world money supply consists of 12,000 clams, and k equals 2. Describe international monetary equilibrium and illustrate with a diagram analogous to Figure 8.1 in the textbook. Suppose the world money supply increases to 18,000 clams; calculate the effect on your answer and illustrate the change in your diagram. Do the same if instead the terms of trade were to alter so that 150 zingoes exchange for 3 poobahs.

Answers to Self-Test

1. 1.1.

2. True.

2. The Automatic Adjustment Process

Basic Ideas

1. The automatic adjustment process is concerned with the way in which the equilibrium described in the previous section is attained.

2. There are three constituents of the automatic adjustment process.

   a. The quantity theory of money determines the equilibrium allocation of the world's money supply among countries, as discussed in the first section of this chapter.

b. Disequilibrium allocations generate payments imbalances, in ways to be examined subsequently.

c. The payments imbalances redistribute money supplies among countries so as to attain the equilibrium allocation.

3. There are two implications of the automatic adjustment process.

a. Payments imbalances are caused by monetary misallocations among countries and serve to correct these misallocations; thus they are temporary.

b. Individual countries cannot pursue independent monetary policies, except transitorily.

4. Be sure you understand: **The Rules of the Game; the sense in which countries cannot have independent monetary policies.**

Self-Test

1. What are "The Rules of the Game"?

2. True or false: The classical automatic adjustment process states that national monetary authorities have little scope for independent action because the classical writers thought the authorities would usually do something stupid.

Solutions to Problems from the Text

8.6 *As in Problem 8.1, America produces 1,000 wheat, Europe 600 cloth, and in equilibrium 5 wheat exchange for 1 cloth. Initially, the world money supply consists of 2,000 gold coins, and k = 1/2. Now suppose that the world money supply increases to 4,000 coins, with the increase taking place in America. Calculate the cumulative payments imbalances necessary to restore equilibrium.*

A cumulative American deficit (or cumulative European surplus) of 1,500.

8.7 *In Problem 8.6, suppose that the American money supply remains equal to 2,000 gold coins, but that economic growth in America raises wheat production to 2,000 units. Calculate the cumulative payments imbalance necessary to restore equilibrium.*

A cumulative American surplus (or cumulative European deficit) of 300.

8.8 *Suppose that, in Problem *8.4, Portuguese tastes permanently change so that each Portuguese now spends one-fourth of her income on cloth and three-fourths on wine. Find the new monetary equilibrium and calculate the cumulative payments im- balances necessary in order to reach this new equilibrium from the old one.*

No payments imbalances are necessary. The Portuguese shift their pattern of production to 91 cloth and 2.25 wine and the new equilibrium is attained, with the same money supplies and prices as the old.

*8.9 *Show how the discussion in this section of the textbook changes if the French, instead of doubling their money supply just once, double it every year forever.*

The French will experience a permanent balance of payments deficit.

Additional Problems

1. In Additional Problem 2 in section 1 above, suppose that the increase in the world's money supply is brought about by money creation in Gormengast. Calculate the cumulative payments imbalances necessary to restore equilibrium.

2. In Problem *8.4, calculate the cumulative payments imbalances necessary to restore equilibrium after England's labor force increases from 100 to 1,000.

Answers to Self-Test

1. The monetary authorities in a country experiencing a balance of payments deficit should allow that country's money supply to fall by at least the amount of the deficit, and the monetary authorities in a country experiencing a balance of payments surplus should allow that country's money supply to rise by at least the amount of the surplus.

2. False.

3. The Balance of Payments and the Domestic Banking System

Basic Ideas

1. This section concerns the mechanics of payments settlements and imbalances with modern banking systems.

2. The basic agents in each country are the public, the commercial banks, and the central bank.

3. Each agent has assets and liabilities, with the excess of the former over the latter equal to net worth.

4. The public's assets consist of deposits in the commercial banks and other assets, and their liabilities are loans from the commercial banks.

5. The assets of the commercial banks are the loans to the public and their reserves (on deposit with the central bank), and their liabilities are the deposits of the public.

6. The assets of the central bank are government bonds and international reserves; their liabilities are the reserves of the commercial banks.

7. The commercial banks are required to hold reserves equal to some fraction of deposits.

8. A balance of payments deficit (surplus) will be reflected by an equal reduction (increase) in the central bank's stock of international reserves, and the commercial banks' reserves with the central bank. This will require, for the reserve requirement to be met, a larger reduction (increase) in deposits at commercial banks, and in those banks' loans to the public.

Solutions to Problems from the Text

8.10 *Work through the example in the textbook if the French reserve requirement is one-tenth rather than one-fifth (keep the German equal to one-fifth).*

The demand deposits of the French public in the French commercial banks would have decreased from fr5,000 to fr4,000.

8.11 *Suppose that in Italy the money supply is 300,000 lire while the Spanish money supply equals 60,000 pesetas. In each country money is in the form of paper notes, but the central bank will exchange its money on demand for gold. In Spain the central bank will buy or sell pesetas for 2 ounces of gold each, and the Italian central bank will exchange a half ounce of gold for each lira. Each central bank has 50,000 ounces of gold in its international reserves. Suppose that Italy experiences a balance of payments deficit of 40,000 lire, and Spain accordingly has a surplus of 10,000 pesetas. Describe what happens, and calculate the money supplies and international reserve stocks in the two countries after the payments imbalance takes place.*

After the imbalance takes place, Italy has a money supply of 260,000 lire and international reserves equal to 30,000 ounces of gold, while Spain has a money supply of 70,000 pesetas and international reserves equal to 70,000 ounces of gold.

8.12 *In Problem 8.11, suppose that Italian law or custom guarantees that at all times the size of the Italian money supply equals exactly 6 lire for each ounce of gold contained in the international reserves of the Italian central bank. How does your answer to Problem 8.11 change?*

The Spanish surplus is 10,000 pesetas or 20,000 ounces. Thus the Spanish gold stock increases to 70,000 ounces and the Spanish money supply to 70,000 pesetas. Italian reserves fall to 30,000 ounces and the Italian money supply falls to 180,000 lire.

8.13 *Suppose, in Problems 8.11 and 8.12, that each central bank initially has a stock of reserves equal to 50,000 dollars, that the Italian central bank will exchange 2 lire for a dollar, and that*

the Spanish central bank will exchange a peseta for 2 dollars.
How do your answers change?

Replace "ounce of gold" by "dollar."

Additional Problems

1. Using Federal Reserve data (see Appendix II of the textbook for data sources), try to compile a table for the United States, as close as possible to Table 8.1 in the textbook, for the beginning of 1987.

2. Answer the analog to the preceding problem for Canada.

4. The Rules of the Game and Monetary Policy

Basic Ideas

1. This section discusses the third ingredient of the automatic adjustment process (the Rules of the Game): payments deficits should reduce a nation's money supply and surpluses should increase it.

2. National monetary authorities often attempt to maintain independent monetary policies by *sterilizing* payments imbalances, that is, by creating new money to replace that lost through a payments deficit or by contracting the money supply to eliminate that acquired through a payments surplus. Thus sterilization means violating the Rules of the Game.

3. Successful sterilization allows a country to control its own money supply, but it also prevents (or retards) payments imbalances from redistributing money between countries. Thus it prevents those imbalances from being self correcting.

4. There are two limitations to the ability of a country to sterilize payments imbalances.

   a. *Central bank assets*: a deficit country, for example, will eventually run out of reserves if it does not first allow the payments imbalance to be corrected.

   b. *Offsetting capital movements*: a deficit country which creates additional money, for example, will find that its residents increase their purchase of foreign assets, so that the sterilization enlarges the size of the deficit. The extent of this offset depends upon the degree of capital mobility. With perfect capital mobility sterilization will be entirely offset, so that it will only magnify payments imbalances and will not enable countries to control their money supplies.

5. Sterilization, or attempted sterilization, has been quite common in practice.

1. True or false: Countries with very large stocks of international reserves are likely to be able to force the burden of adjustment to payments imbalances onto those countries with small stocks of international reserves.

2. Why should a rise in the degree of international capital mobility cause countries to abandon fixed exchange rates?

3. Multiple choice: An increase in the degree of capital mobility can be expected to cause countries to:
    3.1. Need fewer international reserves because private capital movements could substitute for official ones.
    3.2. Want fewer reserves because they would be better able to borrow abroad should a crisis arise.
    3.3. Want more reserves to be better able to counter increased offsetting capital flows.
    3.4. All of the above.
    3.5. None of the above.

Solutions to Problems from the Text

8.14 *In Problem 8.11, suppose that the Italian central bank sterilizes completely the Italian deficit, and that there is no offset. How do your answers change? What are the changes in the bond holdings of the Italian public? The Italian central bank? How do your answers change if the Spanish authorities also fully sterilize the Spanish surplus?*

The Italian money supply remains equal to 300,000 lire, the Italian public has fewer bonds—and the central bank more bonds—by an amount equal in value to 40,000 lire.

8.15 *Suppose, in Problem 8.14, that the Italian authorities completely sterilize and the Spanish do not sterilize at all. Suppose also that one-half of any Italian sterilization is offset by a purchase of foreign bonds: whenever the Italian central bank buys two lire worth of bonds from the Italian public, the public then buys one lira's worth of bonds from abroad. How do your answers to Problem 8.13 change? How do they change if, instead, three-fourths of any sterilization is offset?*

The Italian money supply remains equal to 300,000 lire, the public has 40,000 lire's worth of fewer bonds, the central bank has 80,000 lire's worth of additional bonds, the total Italian payments deficit has been 80,000 lire, and central bank reserves have fallen by 40,000 dollars.

Additional Problems

1. Complete the analog for Germany of Table 8.5 in the textbook, assuming alternatively that:

a. The German central bank attempts to sterilize its surplus.

b. The German central bank does not attempt to sterilize its surplus.

2. Sterilization is simply monetary control motivated by the balance of payments, so any method of monetary control can be used for sterilization. The text discussed open-market operations; alternative methods are changes in reserve requirements and in discount rates. How would the latter two be used to sterilize the effects of a deficit? Rework the example of Tables 8.4 and 8.5 if the French authorities try to sterilize by changing reserve requirements rather than by open-market operations.

Answers to Self-Test

1. True.

2. In order to maintain control over their own money supplies after the increase in offsetting capital flows makes sterilization more difficult.

3. 3.3.

5. Reserve Currencies

Basic Ideas

1. A reserve currency is one which other countries hold in their international reserves. The U.S. dollar is the most important example.

2. If other countries respond to surpluses or deficits by adding to or subtracting from their holdings of a reserve currency, then payments imbalances of the reserve currency country:

a. Do not change that country's stock of international reserves, since the country need not use its reserves to purchase its currency;

b. Change the total world stock of reserves, by an amount equal to its own payments imbalance;

c. Are automatically sterilized, since foreign central banks will hold their reserves of that country's currency in the form of interest earning assets.

Solutions to Problems from the Text

8.17 *The textbook showed that imbalances of a reserve-currency country could be automatically sterilized. But sterilization will be offset, to some degree, if capital is internationally mobile. Suppose that foreign central banks hold reserves only in the form of U.S. dollars. What does this imply about a U.S. balance of payments deficit if there is partial mobility of capital between the United States and the rest of the world? If capital is per-*

fectly mobile? How do your answers change if foreign central banks always hold half of their international reserves in the form of dollars and half in the form of gold?

With capital mobility, the automatic sterilization of U.S. deficits magnifies the size of those deficits, to an extent depending on the degree of capital mobility. Perfect mobility would render automatic sterilization impossible and/or force down interest rates worldwide. If foreign central banks held half of their reserves in the form of gold, only one-half of any U.S. deficits would be automatically sterilized. If the United States does not attempt to sterilize the other half, and if capital mobility is perfect, U.S. deficits will be twice as large as they would be without the automatic sterilization.

8.18 *In Figure 8.4 in the textbook, suppose that France supplies a reserve currency for the rest of the world. Show what happens if the French increase their money supply and the rest of the world sterilizes its own imbalances; if the rest of the world does not sterilize; if the rest of the world tries to increase its money supply.*

Suppose that France is initially at point A in Figure 8.4 and increases its money supply by AH. If the rest of the world consciously sterilizes its own surpluses, and if the French deficits are automatically sterilized, the world remains at D. If the rest of the world does not sterilize its surpluses, the world moves to point B, assuming again that the French deficits are automatically sterilized.

Additional Problems

1. How does your answer to Problem 8.11 change if the Spanish authorities add to their reserves any lire acquired through payments surpluses, instead of holding all their reserves in the form of gold?

2. How does your answer to Problem 8.14 change if the Spanish authorities add to their reserves any lire acquired through payments surpluses, instead of holding all their reserves in the form of gold?

6. Review Questions

1. Write an essay on sterilization. Be sure you discuss what it is, why it has been done, what limits it, and practical experience.

2. What are the basic constituents and implications of the automatic adjustment process?

3. Discuss the importance of the degree of international capital mobility for a fixed exchange rate system.

CHAPTER 9   Open-Economy Macroeconomics

1. Basic Income-Expenditure Theory

Basic Ideas

1. This section is simply a review of basic multiplier theory. If you have any difficulty at all, you should consult the textbook used in your principles course.

2. Be sure you recall and understand: **multiplier, marginal propensity to save.**

Solutions to Problems from the Text

9.1 *Suppose in England consumption equals 100 units plus three-fourths of the English income. What is the English multiplier? What is English income if investment equals 200 units? How much does income increase if investment increases to 300? Answer this by the method of successive rounds, calculating the increase in income after 6 or 7 rounds.*

Multiplier $= 1/MPS = 1/(1 - [3/4]) = 4$. If investment is 200, income $= 1,200$; if investment is 300, income is 1,600.

*9.2 *We can investigate the stability of the equilibrium in Figure 9.1 in the textbook. Suppose that investment is OI_0 but that income is OI_1, so that saving exceeds investment. Then some output is not being sold, so we would expect firms to cut back production. This suggests the disequilibrium hypothesis: Y is falling when S exceeds I and rising when I exceeds S. Is the equilibrium in Figure 9.1 stable? Draw an unstable equilibrium. What is the stability condition?*

The equilibrium in Figure 9.1 is stable, as the stability condition is simply that $MPS > 0$. Thus for an unstable equilibrium, the S line in the figure would have to be downward sloping.

Additional Problems

1. Spanish consumption always equals 500 plus one-half of any income above 500 plus one-fourth of any income above 1,000. What are the

Spanish marginal propensity to save and the Spanish multiplier at all income levels?

2. In the above problem, suppose that investment I is not completely autonomous, as in the discussion in the textbook, but rather equals the sum of an autonomous component plus one-eighth of national income. What is the Spanish multiplier at each income level?

2. The Demand for Imports

Basic Ideas

1. In an open economy, the equilibrium level of national income is that for which $S + M = I + X$.

2. X is regarded as autonomous spending, like I, while M depends upon income, like S.

3. The simple Keynesian theory introduced in this part of the chapter makes four basic assumptions:

   a. The prices of goods are fixed by producers in terms of their own currency.

   b. Fixed exchange rates.

   c. No international capital movements except for official intervention.

   d. Payments imbalances are completely sterilized.

4. Terms to know: **marginal propensity to import, average propensity to import.**

Self-Test

1. Multiple choice: in a certain country, $MPM > APM$. If the country experiences a rise in income, the APM will:
   1.1. Rise.
   1.2. Fall.
   1.3. Remain unchanged.
   1.4. Can't tell without more information.

2. How would an increase in the European demand for American wheat affect the U.S. import curve?

Solutions to Problems from the Text

9.3 *Suppose that English imports always equal 50 units plus one-fourth of English income. Draw the English import function, and calculate the marginal propensity to import, average propensity to import, and the income elasticity of imports.*

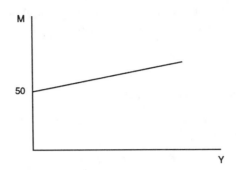

$MPM = 1/4; APM = (1/4) + (50/Y); \text{elasticity} = 1/[1 + 200/Y)]$.

9.4 *Portugal always spends one-half of its income on imports. Draw the Portuguese import curve and calculate the marginal propensity to import, average propensity to import, and income elasticity of imports.*

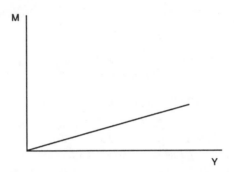

$MPM = 1/2; APM = 1/2; \text{elasticity} = 1$.

Additional Problem

Spain exports goats and imports olives. The Spanish always consume 3 goats with each barrel of olives. If a goat costs 100 pesetas and a barrel of olives costs 150, what is the Spanish marginal propensity to import? How does your answer change if the price of olives increases to 200 pesetas?

Answers to Self-Test

1. 1.1.

2. No effect.

3. Case Study: Mexico, France, and Other Countries

Basic Ideas

1. Import curves vary substantially from country to country, depending upon such things as country size, willingness to trade, income, etc.

2. Be sure you understand: **the difficulty in inferring the value of the MPM from trade and income data.**

Solutions to Problems from the Text

9.5 *Describe the effect of each of the following on a country's import curve.*

    a. *The country imposes a tax on imports.*

    b. *The country's residents decide to save less, thereby boosting income and imports.*

    c. *The country establishes an import quota, prohibiting imports above a certain amount, M*.*

    d. *The rest of the world imposes a tax upon imports from this country.*

    a. The import curve becomes flatter and shifts down.

    b. The import curve shifts up.

    c. The import curve becomes flat when M equals the quota amount, but is unchanged before that.

    d. No effect on the import curve of this country.

9.6 *Using the 1985 U.S. APM of .1 and the estimate of the U.S. income elasticity shown in Table 9.2 in the textbook, calculate an estimate of the U.S. MPM. Calculate the actual increase in U.S. imports for 1985–86 as a fraction of the actual U.S. increase in GNP (see Appendix II of the textbook for data sources). Compare the two results. List all the reasons you can think of why they might differ from each other and from the true MPM. Do the same for Canada.*

Estimate of $MPM = 1.7 \times .1 = .17$.

4. The Simple Foreign Trade Multiplier

Basic Ideas

1. The total of exports and investment determines equilibrium levels of income and of the balance of trade simultaneously. Thus policies which influence one of the latter influence the other as well.

2. The multiplier, which measures the change in Y brought about by a change in X and/or I, is larger the smaller are MPM and MPS.

Self-Test

1. Which of the following policies, if undertaken by the home government, would not affect the home foreign trade multiplier?
   1.1. A tax on imports from abroad.
   1.2. A tax credit for domestic investment.
   1.3. A tax exemption for interest income.
   1.4. An export subsidy.

2. Would the multiplier for the state of California be greater or less than that for the United States as a whole?

Solutions to Problems from the Text

9.7 *Use the method of successive rounds to derive the foreign trade multiplier.*

$$Y_1 - Y_0 = [I_1 - I_0] + [1 - MPS - MPM][I_1 - I_0]$$
$$+ [1 - MPS - MPM]^2[I_1 - I_0] + \ldots$$
$$= \frac{[I_1 - I_0]}{[MPS + MPM]} .$$

9.8 *Find the multiplier for England if consumption equals 100 units plus three-fourths of English income and if imports equal 50 units plus one-fourth of income. What is English income if investment equals 200 units and exports 100? If investment increases to 300? Suppose instead that investment remains at 200 but trade policy is used so that English imports now equal 40 plus one-fifth of English income; calculate the effect on income.*

$MPS = 1/4$; $MPM = 1/4$; multiplier = 2. Income initially equals 700; after the rise in investment, it equals 900. With trade policy the multiplier is 20/9 and the new income is instead 800.

9.9 *Suppose that the Portuguese always save one-quarter of their income and spend one-half on imports. Calculate the multiplier. What is Portuguese income if investment equals 50 and exports 100?*

Multiplier = 4/3. $Y = 200$.

9.10 *Calculate a formula for the term that must be multiplied by a change in I to obtain the effect on the trade balance X − M.*

$-[MPM/(MPM + MPS)]$.

9.11 *The discussion in the textbook assumed that autonomous expenditure was all devoted to domestic goods. Suppose instead that the fraction MPM of an increase in I is spent on imports. Calculate the formula for the multiplier in this case. How would your answer to Problem 9.10 above change?*

$$\left[\frac{(1 - MPM)}{(MPM + MPS)}\right]; -\left[\frac{MPM(1 + MPS)}{(MPM + MPS)}\right].$$

9.12 *The discussion of trade policy assumed that the reduction in M for any Y was all spent on domestic goods, that is, that trade policy switched expenditure from foreign goods to domestic ones. Suppose instead that the income no longer spent on foreign goods is simply saved. How would trade policy affect income and the trade balance in this case?*

Trade policy has no effect on income, and the trade balance is affected by an amount equal to the direct impact of the trade policy.

Additional Problems

1. In the Additional Problem in section 2 of this chapter, suppose that the Spanish always save one-tenth of their income. Calculate the Spanish multiplier both before and after the price rise.

2. Suppose that the foreign country institutes a subsidy on exports to our country. Depict geometrically the effect on domestic income and the trade balance.

Answers to Self-Test

1. 1.2 and 1.4.

2. Less.

*5. Exploring Further: General Equilibrium

Basic Ideas

1. Domestic income depends upon exports, which depend upon foreign income, and foreign income depends upon foreign exports, which depend upon domestic income. Thus domestic and foreign income are jointly determined.

2. An increase in autonomous spending at home will increase imports, since income goes up, and this will increase foreign income. This causes foreign imports to rise, which in turn increases domestic income again, and so on. Exact expressions for the multipliers must take such "secondary repercussions" into account.

3. An increase in autonomous spending at home increases foreign income, and vice-versa. Thus there are "cross multipliers" to be taken account of.

Solutions to Problems from the Text

9.14 *Using the method of successive rounds, derive the multiplier that relates changes in Y^F to changes in I^F when all repercussions are accounted for.*

$$(Y_1^F - Y_0^F) = (I_1^F - I_0^F)$$

$$\times \left\{ 1 + \left[(1 - MPM^F - MPS^F) + \frac{(MPM^F MPM^G)}{(MPM^G + MPS^G)} \right] \right.$$

$$\left. + \left[(1 - MPM^F - MPS^F) + \frac{(MPM^F MPM^G)}{(MPM^G + MPS^G)} \right]^2 + \dots \right\}$$

$$= (I_1^F - I_0^F)$$

$$\times \left[\frac{(MPM^G + MPS^G)}{(MPS^G MPS^F + MPM^G MPS^F + MPS^G MPM^F)} \right].$$

9.15 *Using the method of successive rounds, derive the multiplier that relates changes in Y^F to changes in I^G when all repercussions are accounted for.*

The "cross multiplier" is:

$$\frac{MPM^G}{(MPS^G MPS^F + MPM^G MPS^F + MPS^G MPM^F)}.$$

9.16 *In England consumption equals 100 units plus 3/4 of GNP and imports equal 50 units plus 1/4 of GNP. England trades with Portugal, where savings are 1/4 of GNP and imports are 1/2 of GNP. Calculate multipliers for each country. What is each country's GNP if English investment equals 200 units and Portuguese investment equals 50 units? Calculate the effects of each of the following:*

a. An increase in English I to 300.

b. An increase in Portuguese I to 100.

c. A shift in the English import curve to 40 units plus 1/5 of GNP. Show how your answers illustrate the use of the formulas you derived in Problems 9.14 and 9.15.

In England the direct multiplier is 3 and the cross multiplier is 2; in Portugal the direct multiplier is 2 and the cross multiplier is 1. Initially, English income is 950 and Portuguese income is 450. Thus a rise in English investment to 300 will increase English income to 1,250 and Portuguese income to 650. Alternatively, a rise in Portuguese investment to 100 would raise Portuguese income to 550 and English income to 1,050.

6. Income Adjustment

1. In a Keynesian context, an increase in the domestic money supply will reduce savings, S, and/or increase investment, I, so that $S - I$ falls.

2. This causes an increase in domestic aggregate demand, in an amount determined by the foreign trade multiplier.

3. The rise in aggregate demand causes a rise in imports, in an amount determined by the marginal propensity to consume, and thereby induces a payments deficit. Thus both aggregate demand and the balance of payments deficit increase.

4. The rest of the world experiences an increase in aggregate demand also, but a reduction in its payments deficit.

5. The balance of trade, or excess of exports over imports, can equivalently be defined as the excess of national income over absorption. This reflects a macroeconomic point of view.

6. A depreciation of the exchange rate, by switching demand from foreign goods to domestic goods, increases aggregate demand.

7. The increase in aggregate demand increases the demand for imports and thereby nullifies at least part of the increase in the trade balance brought about by the depreciation.

8. If the economy is initially operating at full capacity, it cannot produce the additional goods demanded as a result of the depreciation, and so there will instead be domestic inflation that will continue until the other effects of the depreciation are nullified.

Self-Test

1. True or false: "Absorption" refers to the money acquired by a country as a result of a balance of payments surplus.

2. In a Keynesian context, what will be the consequences of exchange depreciation by a country operating at full capacity?

3. In a Keynesian context, what will be the consequences of exchange depreciation by a country operating with excess capacity?

4. In a Keynesian context, what will be the consequences of exchange depreciation by a country operating with unemployment and an excessive balance of payments surplus?

Solutions to Problems from the Text

9.17 *How does the discussion in the text change if the home country is so small that the flow of money abroad brought about by the home balance of payments deficit has no significant effect on the rest of the world? Show the final equilibrium in Figure 9.11 in the textbook.*

The $X - M$ line does not now shift up in response to the flow of money abroad, so that the new equilibrium is attained only when the $S - I$ line shifts all the way back to its initial position. Thus the initial domestic income level will eventually be restored.

9.18 *Suppose that domestic residents suddenly decide to save more than before at each level of income. Discuss the consequences. Do the same if instead domestic goods become more attractive to foreigners, so that exports rise.*

The $S - I$ line shifts up, producing consequences just the reverse of those described in the text. In the second case, the $X - M$ line shifts up instead.

9.19 *Suppose the French suddenly acquire an enhanced taste for German goods. Analyze how the exchange rate must adjust to maintain balance of payments equilibrium.*

The franc must depreciate.

9.20 *Suppose that a country is initially at full employment and levies a tariff. Discuss the effects on the balance of trade and on aggregate demand, at the initial exchange rate. How must the exchange rate be altered to keep the balance of trade unchanged?*

The tariff would induce a trade surplus and an increase in aggregate demand; they could be prevented by an appreciation of the currency.

9.21 *Does it matter whether the axes in Figure 9.12 in the textbook are measured in terms of domestic currency or of foreign currency? Why?*

No, as long as both axes are measured in terms of the same currency.

*9.22 *Must the discussion of Figure 9.12 in the textbook be altered if the demand for imports is price inelastic?*

Yes; the conclusions would be reversed.

Additional Problem

Suppose that domestic residents suddenly decide to save more than before at each level of income. Discuss the consequences for the exchange rate, if the balance of trade is to remain unchanged. Do the same if instead domestic goods become more attractive to foreigners, so that exports rise.

Answers to Self-Test

1. False.

2. Inflation, and nothing else.

3. A rise in national income and an improvement in the trade balance.

4. A reduction of unemployment but a worsening of the surplus.

7. The Aggregate Demand Curve

Basic Ideas

1. An aggregate demand curve records what the equilibrium level of aggregate demand will be in a country at each value of the country's price level.

2. A reduction in the price level causes the national money supply to be worth more in real terms and also causes domestic goods to be cheaper relative to foreign goods. This causes aggregate demand to rise; thus the aggregate demand curve has a downward slope.

3. An aggregate demand curve is drawn for fixed values of the money supply, the exchange rate, and the foreign price level. Thus a change in any of these *shifts* the curve.

4. If the equilibrium level of aggregate demand is unequal to aggregate supply, the price level will eventually begin to adjust. This causes the economy to move *along* its aggregate demand curve.

5. Full macroeconomic equilibrium is given by the intersection of the aggregate demand and aggregate supply curves. At this price level there will be no pressure on prices for further adjustments.

Self-Test

1. For each of the following disturbances, write an "*M*" if it will cause a movement along a country's aggregate demand curve, and/or an "*S*" if it will cause a shift of that curve.
   1.1. Depreciation of the exchange rate.
   1.2. A growth of productive capacity.
   1.3. An increase in the foreign price level.
   1.4. An increase in the domestic price level.

2. An aggregate demand curve shows how much an economy will demand at each price level, but this quantity will not actually be produced unless the economy is also on its aggregate supply curve.

Solutions to Problems from the Text

9.23 *Use the aggregate demand curve to discuss the effects of a fall in the price of oil, assuming a fixed exchange rate. How does your analysis change with a floating rate? In each case discuss how monetary policy might be used to respond to the price fall.*

Oil is an imported good, so a reduction in its price reduces the foreign price level relative to the home level and can therefore be expected to shift the home aggregate demand curve to the left. Also oil is an intermediate good, giving it added weight in the home price level, which therefore also falls. However, in the short run demand for oil is relatively unresponsive to price changes. If the economy continues to import the same quantity, it will now cost less. Thus the short-run effect of the price decline will be like an increase in income, shifting the aggregate demand curve to the right.

9.24 *What happens to the balance of trade surplus as we move down and to the right along a country's aggregate demand curve? Explain your answer.*

The increase in aggregate demand causes imports to rise and therefore reduces the balance of trade surplus, but the reduction in the domestic price level makes home goods cheaper relative to foreign goods, and this tends to increase the trade surplus. Whether the surplus actually rises or falls depends on which effect is the stronger.

9.25 *The three lines in Figure 9.15 divide the plane into six regions. Describe how the economy will behave in each of these regions.*

Suppose, for example, that the world is in zone I in the figure below. Then inflation will eventually arise in both France and Germany. Thus each economy will be moving upwards and to the left along its aggregate demand curve. Also German prices are rising more rapidly than French. Thus the German aggregate demand curve will be shifting to the left and the French curve will be shifting to the right. Behavior in the other zones can be described analogously.

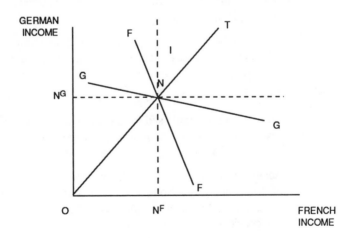

Additional Problems

1. Discuss the short-run and long-run effects of an increased propensity to invest, using aggregate demand and supply curves.

2. Discuss the effects on the domestic economy of a constant rate of foreign inflation.

1. 1.1. *M, S*

    1.2. *M*

    1.3. *M, S*

    1.4. *M*

2. False.

8. International Price Linkages

Basic Ideas

1. Prices in an open economy are influenced by international conditions as well as domestic conditions.

2. The prices of standardized traded goods have the strongest international linkages. Domestic conditions cannot force them to depart from foreign prices, and exchange rate changes are offset by price changes.

3. The prices of nontraded goods have the weakest international linkages. They are not influenced directly by foreign conditions or by exchange rate variations.

4. The prices of differentiated traded goods are in between in terms of their international linkages.

5. The time horizon also matters. Domestic prices are more likely to move in line with foreign prices when more time is allowed for adjustment.

6. The Law of One Price has two versions:

    a. Identical goods should sell for the same price in different countries (except for tariffs, transportation costs, etc.), once the exchange rate is used to compare prices expressed in different currencies.

    b. Relative prices are determined by real considerations independently of the exchange rate, so that any change in the latter should be accompanied by offsetting changes in the prices of goods, unless real considerations also change.

7. If the Law of One Price holds, Purchasing Power Parity will be observed: the depreciation of a nation's currency will just equal the excess of inflation in that nation above inflation abroad.

8. Purchasing Power Parity is in fact often violated, but it does seem to be partly true.

9. Terms to know: **Law of One Price, Purchasing Power Parity, real exchange rate, effective exchange rate.**

1. Multiple choice: The price of which of the following goods is most tightly linked to foreign prices?
   1.1. Automobiles.
   1.2. Iron ore.
   1.3. Haircuts.
   1.4. Construction.
   1.5. Peanut butter.

2. Multiple choice: The price of which of the following goods is most tightly linked to foreign prices?
   2.1. Consumer goods.
   2.2. Services.
   2.3. Producer goods.
   2.4. All of the above.
   2.5. None of the above.

3. True or false: Purchasing Power Parity implies that exchange depreciation is caused by differences in inflation rates across countries.

4. True or false: Purchasing Power Parity implies that differences in inflation rates across countries are caused by exchange depreciation.

Solutions to Problems from the Text

9.26 *What will Table 9.1 look like if the initial disturbance is cost inflation in the United States rather than a depreciation of the dollar? That is, suppose that initially all prices are $100 and both exchange rates are $1.00, and that the price of foreign currency remains $1.00 throughout. Instead, an increase in the U.S. money supply, for example, causes a 50 percent rise in all wages and costs, but there is no similar change abroad. Indicate the responses, and explain your answer.*

		Short-run response	Medium-run response	Long-run response
Price of foreign currency		$1.00	$1.00	$1.00
Standardized	U.S.	$100	$100	$100
traded goods	Foreign	$100	$100	$100
Differentiated	U.S.	$125	$111	$100
traded goods	Foreign	$100	$100	$100
Nontraded goods	U.S.	$150	$125	$100
U.S. price index		$125	$112	$100
Real exchange rate		.80	.89	1.00
Price of traded goods relative to nontraded		.71	.82	1.00

9.27 *In Table 9.3, calculate the July 1986 average values of four bilateral exchange rates for South Korea. Calculate the South Korean effective exchange rate, using the following weights: yen, 50 percent; US$, 30 percent; DM, 10 percent; C$, 10 percent. Using data in Table 9.2 to approximate inflation differentials, calculate the South Korean real exchange rate.*

CANADIAN $	123
JAPANESE ¥	208
W GERMAN DM	123
US $	146
EFFECTIVE	172
REAL	155

Additional Problem

This section discussed changes in three types of price indices: the overall price index, the price of home-produced traded goods relative to foreign goods, and the price of traded goods relative to nontraded goods. On the basis of Table 9.3, speculate how each of these behaved in the United States during 1980–86.

Answers to Self-Test

1. 1.2.

2. 2.3.

3. False.

4. False.

9. Relative Price Adjustment: The Elasticity Approach

Basic Ideas

1. This section looks at the relation of relative price changes and exchange rate changes and at the role of relative price changes in the adjustment process. The terms of trade is the relative price examined.

2. An appreciation of one country's currency raises the prices of that country's goods relative to foreign goods. In response, imports rise and exports fall.

3. An increase in the money supply—or a decrease in the demand for money—in one country raises the prices of that country's goods relative to foreign goods. In response, imports rise and exports fall.

4. The trade price elasticities determine the size of the response to the price changes.

5. The analysis of this section of the textbook is more relevant the less rigid is the link between foreign and domestic prices.

6. The response of importers and exporters to the relative price change produced by a depreciation is often delayed, but the depreciation immediately increases the domestic-currency cost of imports priced in terms of foreign currency. Thus depreciation often causes the balance of trade to deteriorate before it improves.

7. Be sure to understand: **elasticity of import demand, Marshall-Lerner condition, *J* curve.**

Self-Test

1. True or false: According to the theory of this section, a spontaneous shift in consumer tastes from foreign goods to domestic goods, with a floating exchange rate, would cause an appreciation of the domestic currency that would continue until domestic relative prices became high enough to clear commodity markets.

2. True or false: According to the theory of this section, a spontaneous shift in consumer tastes from foreign goods to domestic goods, with a fixed exchange rate, would induce a balance of payments surplus that would continue until the domestic economy accumulated enough money to raise domestic prices high enough to clear commodity markets.

3. True or false: With floating exchange rates, high elasticities are to be welcomed because they imply that exchange-rate variations will be rare and of modest size.

4. True or false: With a fixed exchange rate, high elasticities are to be welcomed because they imply that payments imbalances will be gradual and of modest size.

Solutions to Problems from the Text

9.29 *When the California Gold Rush began, the prices of ordinary consumer goods and services were driven to very high levels in the mining regions. After a while these prices fell to more normal levels. Discuss in terms of the automatic adjustment process.*

The supply of gold (and the shortage of commodities) pushed up prices in California, leading to a balance of payments deficit. This continued until the outflow of gold (and the inflow of commodities) allowed prices to approximate more nearly those in the rest of the world.

9.30 *Suppose that Italy's income is 10,000 olives, Spain's is 4,000 goats, the equilibrium terms of trade equal 2 olives per goat, and k = 2. Initially Spain's money supply is 80,000 gold coins and Italy's is 100,000 gold coins. Whenever the relative price of goats in terms of olives increases by one olive, the Spanish*

*respond by increasing their imports from Italy by 1,800 olives
and the Italians purchase 900 fewer goats from Spain. Suppose
the Spanish money supply increases by 72,000 gold coins.
Describe in detail the resulting adjustment.*

Initially the price of a goat is 10 gold coins and that of an olive is 5
coins. When Spain's money supply increases from 80,000 coins to
152,000 coins, the price of a goat rises to 19 coins, so that the relative price of goats in terms of olives rises from 2 to 3.8. The Spanish
then increase imports by 3,240 [= 1.8 x 1800] olives and the Italians
reduce their imports from Spain by 1,620 goats. These changes in
trade volumes produce a Spanish balance of payments deficit [Italian
surplus] of 46,980 gold coins [(19 x 1620 + (5 x 3240)]. [*NOTE: The
price changes will also change the values of the initial trade volumes.
But the problem supplies no data on the latter, so assume they are in
fact zero.*] The payments imbalances reduce the Spanish money supply to 105,020 coins, lowering the price of a goat to 13.1 coins, and
increase the Italian money supply to 146,980 coins, raising the price
of an olive to 7.3 coins. Thus the new relative price of goats in terms
of olives is 1.8. The price change causes Spanish imports to fall by
3,600 olives and Italian imports to rise by 1,800 goats; thus Italy
now imports 180 goats and 360 olives for a balance of payments
deficit (Spanish surplus) of 4,986 gold coins. Proceed in this way to
calculate subsequent developments.

9.31 *Suppose again that Italy produces 10,000 olives, Spain 4,000
goats, 2 olives exchange for one goat in equilibrium, k = 2, and
that Spain's money supply consists of 80,000 pesetas and Italy's
of 100,000 lire. Suppose the peseta depreciates by one-half of
its equilibrium value, and that the lire price of olives and the
peseta price of goats are unchanged. What happens?*

The peseta price of olives doubles and the lire price of goats falls by
one-half, so that the price of goats in terms of olives falls by 50
percent. This should increase Spanish exports and reduce Spanish
imports, etc., as discussed in the text.

9.32 *Chapter 8's discussion of the price-specie flow mechanism
assumed, as in equations (8.1) and (8.2) in the textbook, that
the demand for money in each country is proportional to that
country's production of goods. Sometimes it is argued instead
that money demand is proportional to demand for a country's
goods. Can you think of any reason for one to be the case rather
than the other? To see what difference it makes, suppose that
each country consumes only the other country's products, that
is, the French consume only butane and the Germans only
apples. Then French demand for money will be proportional to
(py^G) rather than to y^F, and German money demand will be
proportional to (y^F/p) instead of to y^G. What difference does
this make to the automatic adjustment process?*

In this case an increase in L^F relative to L^G causes p to rise rather than
fall, so that the discussion is reversed.

9.33 *Use the aggregate demand curve to discuss the effects of an increase in the money supply with a floating exchange rate.*

The aggregate demand curve shifts to the right, and the exchange rate depreciates. As domestic inflation develops, the economy moves up along the new curve, with further accompanying depreciation.

*9.34 *The text pointed out that a one percent depreciation increased export receipts by e* percent and reduced import expenses by e − 1 percent. These were then added to conclude that the total improvement in the trade balance would be proportional to e + e* − 1. Actually this addition gives only an approximation that becomes less accurate the larger is the initial trade imbalance. Why is this? Derive the true expression.*

A one percent depreciation reduces import expenses by $e - 1$ percent, as discussed in the text. Export receipts increase by e^* percent, but this should be expressed as a percentage of import expenses—not exports—if we are to add the two together. As a percentage of the latter, export receipts increase by $e^*(X/pM)$ percent. Thus the improvement in the trade balance is proportional to $e^*(X/pM) + e - 1$. If trade is initially balanced, $X = pM$, so this reduces to the expression in the textbook.

Additional Problems

1. How is the analysis of this section of the textbook affected if France is a small country and Germany is the rest of the world?

2. Suppose that the terms of trade is determined entirely by real considerations and that exchange rate changes cannot influence it, but that each country also has a class of nontraded goods, as discussed in the previous section of the textbook. How is the analysis of this section of the text affected?

Answers to Self-Test

1. False.

2. True.

3. False.

4. False.

*10. Exploring Further: Nontraded Goods

Basic Ideas

1. Depreciation increases the price of traded goods relative to nontraded goods.

2. This change in relative prices causes firms to switch production from nontraded goods to traded goods, and consumers switch their purchases from traded goods to nontraded goods.

3. This change in production and consumption reduces the excess demand for traded goods, that is, it reduces the balance of trade deficit.

4. The change also creates an excess demand for nontraded goods. This causes the economy to move up along its aggregate demand curve until the demand for nontraded goods comes into line with the supply.

Solutions to Problems from the Text

9.35 *How does the analysis of this section change if, instead of a depreciation, the exchange rate remains fixed but the domestic money supply is increased?*

The increase in the money supply will promote inflation at home. But with the prices of traded goods held down by world markets, the inflation affects only nontraded goods. Thus the price of nontraded goods rises relative to traded goods. This is just the reverse of the case discussed in the textbook, so it produces just the reverse effects.

9.36 *How does the analysis of this section change if the exchange rate is allowed to float and the domestic money supply is increased?*

In this case the domestic prices of traded goods can also rise if the exchange rate depreciates a like amount. Thus the increase in the money supply causes exchange depreciation rather than an increase in the price of nontraded goods relative to traded goods.

11. Hoarding and Dishoarding: The Monetary Approach

Basic Ideas

1. If residents of a country have larger money balances than they wish, they will begin to dishoard—or spend some of the excess. This induces a balance of payments deficit if the exchange rate is fixed.

2. If residents of a country have smaller money balances than they wish, they will begin to hoard—or spend less than their incomes. This induces a balance of payments surplus if the exchange rate is fixed.

3. Relative price changes play no role in this facet of the automatic adjustment process. But the absolute level of world prices adjusts so that what one country wishes to hoard just matches what the rest of the world wishes to dishoard.

4. If Purchasing Power Parity holds, a depreciation of the domestic currency will require that inflation at home rise relative to inflation

abroad. This will increase the demand for money at home and reduce it abroad.

5. Since domestic residents now have smaller money balances than they wish, they will begin to hoard. Similarly foreign residents will begin to dishoard. In this way the depreciation of the domestic currency increases the domestic balance of payments surplus and reduces the foreign balance of payments surplus.

6. Term to understand: **propensity to hoard**.

Self-Test

1. Multiple choice: According to the mechanism studied in this section, disturbances to equilibrium produce price changes:
   1.1. So that the terms of trade can adjust.
   1.2. To bring reciprocal demand into play.
   1.3. To cause hoarding in one country to just match dishoarding abroad.
   1.4. All of the above.
   1.5. None of the above.

2. True or false: An increase in the money supply of a "small" country would have a big impact on inflation in that country, since it can't influence foreign prices and thereby "export" inflation.

Solutions to Problems from the Text

9.37 *Suppose that Italy's income is equal in value to 10,000 olives and that Spain's consists of 4,000 goats. In equilibrium 2 olives exchange for 1 goat. If the world money supply consists of 180,000 ounces of gold, and if k = 2, what are the equilibrium money supplies and money prices? If a Spanish peseta equals 2 ounces of gold and the Italian lira equals 1/2 ounce of gold, what are the money supplies and money prices in terms of pesetas? In terms of lire?*

$L^S = 80,000$, $L^I = 100,000$, $P_G = 10$ ounces $= 5$ pesetas $= 20$ lire. $P_O = 5$ ounces $= 10$ lire $= 2.5$ pesetas.

9.38 *Suppose, in the previous problem, that Spain obtained 72,000 ounces of additional gold from the New World. How must the money prices of goats and olives change if the Spanish excess supply of money is to just equal the Italian excess demand? Suppose that the propensity to hoard of each individual is such that everyone wants to take exactly ten years to adjust money supply to demand, performing one-tenth of the adjustment each year. What are the Spanish and Italian imbalances in the first year after the Spanish obtain the new gold? What are the new money supplies after one year, and the payments imbalances in the second year? Continue to give answers for succeeding years until the new equilibrium is reached.*

-157-

$P_G = 14$ ounces and $P_O = 7$ ounces. The initial Spanish deficit (Italian surplus) is 4,000 ounces, so that after one year $L^S = 148,000$ ounces and $L^I = 104,000$.

9.39 *In Problem 9.37, suppose Spain and Italy have paper currencies, with 100,000 lire and 80,000 pesetas. What are the equilibrium prices and the exchange rate?*

$P_G = 10$ lire = 10 pesetas; $P_O = 5$ lire = 5 pesetas; and $R =$ one lira per peseta.

9.40 *Suppose, in Problem 9.39 above, that the peseta depreciates relative to the lira, by one half of its equilibrium value. If PPP holds, what must happen to the money prices of the two goods in the two currencies if the excess demand for lire is to equal in value the excess supply of pesetas?*

Now the Italian exchange rate is 1/2 a lira per peseta. $P_G = 140/9$ lire = 280/9 pesetas; $P_O = 35/9$ pesetas = 35/18 lire.

9.41 *The discussion in the textbook showed that exchange deprecia-tion tends to increase domestic inflation relative to foreign inflation. Suppose that some exogenous event causes the domes-tic inflation rate to rise but does not influence foreign inflation. What will be the likely effect on the exchange rate, if the latter is free to adjust? What, in turn, will be the consequences of this adjustment? Compare with the effects of increased domestic inflation when exchange rates are fixed.*

The domestic currency would likely depreciate.

9.42 *Show how Figure 9.20 in the textbook can be used to analyze a depreciation of the franc if both axes are measured in marks.*

In Figure 9.4, instead of the *GG* line shifting out, the *FF* line would shift to the left and become steeper.

9.43 *The text described the response to a monetary disturbance: an increase in the French money supply. Suppose instead that the disturbance is real, say economic growth in Germany in the form of an increase in y^G. Analyze the response using diagrams such as Figure 9.19 in the textbook.*

An increase in y^G increases the German demand for money and therefore shifts the *GG* schedule in Figure 9.21 *downward*. This lowers the world price level and produces a German balance of payments surplus and a corresponding French deficit. These imbalances cause both schedules to rise until their intersection point reaches the *P* axis, when the new equilibrium is attained and the payments imbalances cease.

*9.44 *How do your answers to Problems 9.37 and 9.38 change if the Spanish obtain an additional 72,000 ounces of gold not just once, but each and every year?*

In Problem 9.37 the equilibrium money supplies and money prices continue to increase in tandem (though at a decreasing rate). Spain develops a permanent balance of payments deficit.

Additional Problems

1. In Additional Problem 2 in section 1 of chapter 8, suppose that the increase in the world's money supply is brought about by money creation in Gormengast, and that the residents of each country always wish to eliminate one-half of any discrepancy between money demand and supply in one year. Calculate the consequent payments imbalances for the first three years after the Gormengastian money creation.

2. In Problem *8.4, calculate the payments imbalances in the three years following the increase in England's labor force from 100 to 1,000, if the English always wish to eliminate one-half of any discrepancy between money demand and supply in one year, and the Portuguese always wish to eliminate one-fourth.

3. Suppose that France discovers credit cards, so that k falls in France, but not Germany. Analyze the response using a diagram such as Figure 9.22 in the textbook.

4. In Additional Problem 2 in section 2 of chapter 7, suppose that the residents of each country always wish to eliminate one-half of any discrepancy between money demand and supply in one year. Calculate the consequent exchange-rate changes during the first three years after the Gormengastian money creation, assuming that adjustment takes place entirely through exchange-rate alterations.

Answers to Self-Test

1. 1.3.

2. False.

12. Internal and External Balance under Fixed Exchange Rates

Basic Ideas

1. This section addresses the dilemma faced by national authorities who wish to use expenditure policy to attain simultaneously internal balance (the desired level of aggregate demand) and external balance (the desired size of the balance of payments deficit).

2. If there is international capital mobility, a combination of monetary policy and fiscal policy—the two types of expenditure policy—can be found that will just attain both types of balance at once.

3. The reason is that the two types of policy have differential effects on the two types of balance. Fiscal policy directly influences aggregate demand and, through the multiplier, the balance of trade. Monetary policy does the same but, in addition, it exerts a second effect on the balance of payments, by changing interest rates and thereby influencing the capital account.

4. This argument is true, however, only in the short run. Once individuals have responded to the change in interest rates and undertaken their desired capital transactions, the effect on the capital account will cease.

Self-Test

1. Multiple choice: Under which of the following circumstances would this section's conclusion about how to attain both internal balance and external balance no longer hold?
    1.1. The absence of international capital mobility.
    1.2. Perfect capital mobility.
    1.3. The long run.
    1.4. All of the above.
    1.5. None of the above.

2. True or false: The presence of international capital mobility causes fiscal policy to exert a greater influence on the balance of payments relative to aggregate demand, compared to monetary policy.

Solutions to Problems from the Text

9.45 *The* IB *and* EB *lines in Figure 9.21 in the textbook divide the plane into four zones. What is the interpretation of each of these zones in terms of policy goals?*

In the zone NE of point *A* aggregate demand is excessive and the balance of payments surplus is too high; in SW of point *A* just the reverse is the case. In the zone NW of point *A* aggregate demand is deficient and the balance of payments surplus is too high; in SE of *A* just the reverse is the case.

9.46 *Suppose that savings are small so that the increase in the capital-account surplus caused by a rise in the domestic interest rate almost entirely disappears after the short run. Show what the relative positions of the* IB *and* EB *schedules in Figure 9.21 in the text look like in both the short run and the long run. What do you conclude about policy?*

The diagram would look qualitatively the same, but in the long run points above the *EB* line would correspond to payments deficits because of international interest payments.

9.47 *Suppose that the economy is initially in external balance at point* D *in Figure 9.21 in the text and in order also to attain internal balance the interest rate is reduced by* BD *and the bud-*

get deficit by AB. *Show in the diagram what happens after the short-run change in the capital account disappears, assuming that both the continuing effect on the capital account and the long-run effect on net interest income are small enough to be ignored. Show what additional policy measures the authorities must take in order to preserve internal and external balance.*

The country will develop a larger balance of payments surplus than it wants. To prevent this the authorities must either find an additional policy with which to reconcile internal and external goals, or they must be prepared repeatedly to change monetary and fiscal policies in order to attain the desired short-run effects over and over.

*9.48 *The intersection of the* IB *and* EB *lines in Figure 9.21 in the text gives a specific policy prescription (point A). But in actual situations we will have at best only a very hazy idea of the shape and position of these curves, and so will not know where A is. It is therefore useful to have simple rules for adjusting the targets so as to "grope" toward A. One simple rule would be to assign each instrument to one target. For example, if the interest rate were assigned to internal balance and the budget deficit to external balance, one would reduce the interest rate whenever the economy was in a recession and reduce the budget deficit whenever there was a balance of payments deficit. An alternative assignment would be monetary policy to external balance and fiscal policy to internal balance. Discuss the relative merits of these two assignments as means to attain point A.*

Suppose that the economy is initially at point E in each panel of the following figure.

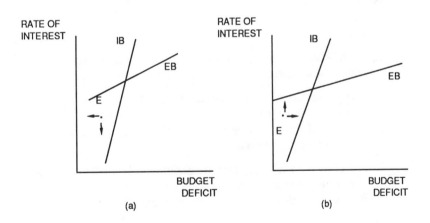

This economy is in a recession and is experiencing a larger balance of payments deficit than the authorities wish. If the authorities assign monetary policy to internal balance and fiscal policy to external balance, they will lower interest rates in response to the recession and reduce the government budget deficit in response to the payments deficit. This is illustrated in panel (a). The result is that the economy moves to the southwest and both problems worsen! The influence of each policy tool on the target it is assigned to is overwhelmed by the influence of the other policy tool. If the authorities instead assign monetary policy to external balance and fiscal policy to internal balance, they will act in the reverse manner to that just described. This is illustrated in panel (b). In this case the policy actions improve matters. The point of this is that if policy tools are to be assigned to particular targets, it is important that each tool be assigned to the target on which it has relatively the most influence, compared to the other tool. Note the analogy with the principle of comparative advantage. In the above figure, the *IB* and *EB* lines divide each panel into four zones. You should verify that if point *E* were instead in the northeast zone, it would still be crucial to properly match tools and targets, but that this is less important in the northwest and southeast zones, where each tool would be used in a particular direction regardless of which target it is aiming at. But even in these cases it is likely that the economy would sooner or later move into one of the zones where the proper assignment becomes vital.

Answers to Self-Test

    1. 1.4.

    2. False.

13. Aggregate Demand Management with Floating Exchange Rates

Basic Ideas

    1. With floating exchange rates, an expansion of the money supply will depreciate the currency and stimulate aggregate demand.

    2. The greater the degree of international capital mobility, the more transitory will be the influence of a monetary expansion on domestic aggregate demand, and the greater will be its depressing influence on foreign aggregate demand.

    3. With floating exchange rates, fiscal policy will be effective in influencing aggregate demand if capital is not very mobile, but will be ineffective with a high degree of capital mobility.

Solutions to Problems from the Text

    9.49 *Suppose that France and Germany have a floating exchange rate, and suppose that there is an exogenous increase in the German desire to consume French goods. What will be the results? How does your answer depend upon the degree of capital mobility? Contrast your answer with what would happen under fixed rates.*

The immediate effect will be to generate a French trade surplus, to stimulate aggregate demand in France, and to depress it in Germany. The changes in aggregate demand will limit the trade surplus, but they will also put upward pressure on French interest rates and downward pressure on German interest rates, thereby inducing a French capital-account surplus. The franc will appreciate enough to cancel these effects.

9.50 *Suppose that France and Germany have a floating exchange rate, and suppose that there is an exogenous increase in the German desire to own French bonds. What will happen? How does your answer depend upon the degree of capital mobility? Contrast your answer with what would happen under fixed rates.*

The immediate effect will be a French capital-account surplus, with downward pressure on French interest rates and the reverse in Germany. This will stimulate French aggregate demand and induce a trade deficit to partially cancel the capital surplus. Exchange rate changes will complete the cancellation.

9.51 *The textbook showed that, with floating exchange rates and perfect capital mobility, monetary policy could influence domestic aggregate demand, but the influence would be temporary. Fiscal policy would have no influence. Is this lack of influence of fiscal policy also temporary? Explain.*

No, because as long as the budget deficit continues new bonds will continually be sold to foreigners.

*9.52 *How are our conclusions about the temporary effect of monetary policy in the presence of capital mobility altered when account is taken of: (a) the fact that there will be continuing capital flows in a growing world with positive net saving, and (b) international payments of interest income?*

(a) In this case there will be a permanent capital-account deficit and therefore also a permanent trade surplus, which will require a depreciated exchange rate and consequent rise in aggregate demand. (b) In this case there will eventually develop a permanent surplus due to interest income from abroad and therefore also a permanent trade deficit, which will require an appreciated exchange rate and consequent reduction in aggregate demand.

Additional Problems

1. The main advantage of floating exchange rates is that they allow countries independent control over their own money supplies. Distinguish this from independent control over their own economic performances.

2. Discuss why countries might want to limit, or to encourage, international capital mobility.

14. Case Study: U.S. Experience in the 1980s

Basic Ideas

1. This section uses the theory presented in the preceding section as a framework to discuss U.S. experience in the 1980s.

2. The U.S. federal government ran a large budget deficit in the early 1980s. The current account developed a large deficit position and the dollar appreciated dramatically. This was followed by a large depreciation in the middle of the decade.

3. The current-account deficit and dollar appreciation can be explained in terms of a downward shift of $S - I$ and $X - M$. Explaining the subsequent depreciation requires us to augment the simple theoretical model.

Solutions to Problems from the Text

9.53 *When large federal budget deficits began to develop in the early 1980s, many commentators expected them to ignite a burst of inflation. But this did not happen; in fact, the inflation rate fell. Explain in terms of our theory.*

Commentators expected that the deficits would add to the demand for U.S. goods and thus push prices up. But instead much of the added demand was satisfied by imports, as reflected in the large current-account deficit.

9.54 *How is the discussion of intervention in this chapter sensitive to whether that intervention is sterilized or not?*

The chapter discussed the possibility that intervention to force the dollar down could help finance the U.S. budget deficit, that is, that the deficit would be partly paid for with new dollars. This presumes that the intervention is not sterilized.

Additional Problem

Section 10* of chapter 7 gave an alternative, intertemporal, explanation of the experience discussed in this section. How consistent are the two explanations? Do you prefer one to the other?

15. Floating Exchange Rates

Basic Ideas

1. This section examines the operation of floating exchange rates in a world with capital mobility.

2. Purchasing Power Parity requires a positive relation (the *PPP* line) between the exchange rate and the ratio of domestic prices to foreign prices.

3. Equilibrium in the asset markets (money and bonds, the latter exchanged between countries) implies a negative relation (the *AME* line) between the exchange rate and the ratio of domestic prices to foreign prices.

4. Because asset markets attain equilibrium quickly, the economy must be on the *AME* line even in the short run. In the long run Purchasing Power Parity must also hold, so long-run equilibrium is given by the intersection of the *AME* and *PPP* lines.

5. Monetary disturbances can be depicted as shifts of the *AME* line, so that long-run equilibrium moves along the *PPP* line. But if the exchange rate adjusts more rapidly than commodity prices, the former will "overshoot" its new equilibrium value and then have to backtrack. Thus monetary disturbances would make exchange rates volatile.

6. Real disturbances can be viewed as shifts of the *PPP* line and movements along *AME*. Thus real disturbances would make exchange rates neither more volatile nor less volatile than commodity prices. Purchasing Power Parity would appear to be violated, but only because the equilibrium relation between prices was itself changing.

7. Things to understand: **the AME line and its slope; overshooting; the role and implications of relative speeds of adjustment.**

Self-Test

1. Multiple choice: To maintain equilibrium in the asset markets, a depreciation of the exchange rate would have to be accompanied by:
   1.1. An equal excess of domestic inflation over foreign inflation.
   1.2. A mass resignation of central bankers.
   1.3. An increase in foreign interest rates.
   1.4. An excess of foreign inflation over domestic inflation.
   1.5. None of the above.

2. Multiple choice: To maintain equilibrium in the commodity markets, a depreciation of the exchange rate would have to be accompanied by:
   2.1. An equal excess of domestic inflation over foreign inflation.
   2.2. A mass resignation of central bankers.
   2.3. An increase in foreign interest rates.
   2.4. An excess of foreign inflation over domestic inflation.
   2.5. None of the above.

3. True or false: *Overshooting* of the exchange rate refers to the short-term overreaction, relative to the long-term effect, of the exchange rate to a monetary disturbance that is made necessary by the fact that commodity prices don't adjust for a while, so that in the meantime the exchange rate must overadjust to compensate.

Solutions to Problems from the Text

9.56 *Can the different responses of the exchange rate to monetary and real disturbances help explain why in Table 9.6 in the textbook exchange rates were more volatile than commodity prices but less so than asset prices?*

The theory suggested that exchange rates were as volatile as asset prices (interest rates) in response to monetary shocks, but no more volatile than commodity prices in response to real shocks. Since actual experience presumably includes a mixture of both types of disturbances, this is not inconsistent with the observation that exchange rate volatility has actually been somewhere between that of asset prices and that of commodity prices.

9.57 *The monetary shock analyzed in this section was an unanticipated increase in the home money supply. Suppose instead that the home authorities announce that in one year they will increase the money supply by a certain amount and that everyone believes them, and that they then do so. Discuss the likely consequences.*

With the money supply expected to increase in a year, people would become less willing to hold domestic currency now and the exchange rate would begin now to depreciate gradually in response. This would give commodity prices time to gradually adjust also, so as to preserve commodity market equilibrium. The *AME* curve would gradually shift outward and equilibrium would move along the *PPP* line, reaching the new equilibrium at point *C'* in one year, just as the money supply is actually increased to what everyone had correctly expected it to be.

*9.58 *The discussion in the textbook of the slope of the AME line assumed that people expected the exchange rate to move toward its long-run equilibrium value. Suppose instead that they expect any departure from that value to be accentuated, at least for a while. How might this affect the slope of the AME line and the subsequent analysis?*

In this case the explanation of the slope of the *AME* line given in the textbook is just reversed, and so that line has a positive slope. The following figure shows the effect of an increase in the money supply when the *AME* line is flatter than *PPP* and when it is steeper.

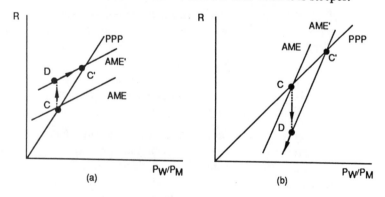

In both panels, the monetary expansion shifts the *AME* line outward to *AME'*, and short-term equilibrium shifts from point *C* to *D*. In panel (a) this does not involve overshooting, the equilibrium sub-sequently moves along *AME'* from *D* to the new long run at equilibrium at *C'*. In this case, however, peoples' expectations are systematically incorrect: since the exchange rate *R* is lower at *D* than at its equilibrium at *C'*, people by assumption expect it to deviate even more, but it does just the opposite.

In panel (b), the short-run adjustment of *R* from *C* to *D* is in the opposite direction to its new equilibrium. From *D*, the exchange rate appreciates even more and moves southwest along *AME'* ever further from *C'*. Equilibrium is unstable, with monetary disturbances causing explosive deviations. However this behavior is consistent with peoples' expectations: at D they expect the exchange rate to move even further from its value at *C'*, and it does.

Additional Problems

1. The discussion in the textbook assumed that the exchange rate adjusted much more rapidly than did commodity prices. Suppose that the opposite was in fact the case. How would responses to monetary and real shocks change?

2. The discussion in the textbook assumed that the asset markets adjusted much more rapidly than did commodity markets. Suppose that the opposite was in fact the case. How would responses to monetary and real shocks change?

Answers to Self-Test

1. 1.4.

2. 2.1.

3. True.

*16. Exploring Further: *IS – LM* Analysis in an Open Economy

Basic Ideas

1. The *IS* curve shows those combinations of the interest rate and national income for which the demand for a country's output just equals that level of income.

2. The *LM* curve shows those combinations of the interest rate and national income for which the demand for a country's money just equals its supply.

3. The *BP* curve shows those combinations of the rate of interest and national income for which a country's balance of payments is in neither deficit nor surplus at the existing level of the exchange rate.

4. The intersection of the *IS* and *LM* curves determines a country's short-run equilibrium interest rate and income. The position of this intersection relative to the *BP* curve determines the payments imbalance.

5. Long-run equilibrium is illustrated by a simultaneous intersection of all three curves.

6. A depreciation of the exchange rate shifts the IS curve to the right and up.

7. A depreciation of the exchange rate shifts the BP curve to the right and down.

Solutions to Problems from the Text

9.59 *How does a rise in the domestic price level affect the LM curve? The BP curve?*

The *LM* curve shifts up, the *IS* curve shifts down, and the *BP* curve shifts up.

9.60 *How is each of the curves affected by a rise in the foreign price level?*

The *IS* curve shifts to the right, the *BP* curve shifts up, and the *LM* curve stays put.

9.61 *Analyze the effects of an exogenous permanent shift in tastes from foreign goods toward domestic goods.*

The *IS* curve shifts to the right, causing the interest rate and income to rise, and the *BP* curve shifts down, indicating a balance of payments surplus. The domestic price level begins to rise, shifting these curves back toward where they were originally. The balance of payments deficit and the rise in domestic prices produce more or less offsetting effects upon the position of the *LM* curve.

9.62 *Analyze the effects of a more expansionary fiscal policy with a fixed exchange rate and also with a floating rate.*

The *IS* curve shifts to the right, increasing the rate of interest and national income, and producing a balance of payments deficit if the exchange rate is fixed. The latter causes the *LM* curve to begin shifting up, further raising the interest rate but gradually forcing income back down. This continues until the three curves again come into a common intersection, when the deficit ceases. The interest rate is higher than originally, reflecting the shift in spending from private investment to the government deficit.

With a floating exchange rate, the expansionary fiscal policy again shifts the *IS* curve to the right. To prevent a deficit, the exchange rate depreciates, shifting the BP curve down and to the right and the IS curve up and to the right.

9.64 *Analyze in detail the effects of an increase in the domestic money supply if the authorities adjust the exchange rate to prevent a balance of payments deficit.*

The increase in the money supply shifts the LM curve down and to the right. To prevent a deficit, the exchange rate depreciates, shifting the BP curve down and to the right and the IS curve up and to the right. In order to keep the balance of payments equal to zero, the curves must shift so that the intersection of the IS and LM curves moves along BP.

9.66 *The discussion in the text on the long-run consequences of depreciation assumed that the money supply remained constant, that is, that all payments imbalances were completely sterilized. How must the discussion change if instead there is no sterilization at all?*

The discussion in the text indicated a payments surplus, so if this is not sterilized it will cause the LM curve to shift down and to the right.

Additional Problems

1. Use IS-LM-BP analysis to restate the discussion, in section 12 of the textbook, of internal and external balance.

2. Use IS-LM-BP analysis to discuss the effects of an increase in the money supply with complete sterilization of all payments imbalances.

3. Use IS-LM-BP analysis to discuss the influence of the degree of international capital mobility on the effectiveness of monetary and fiscal policy, with fixed exchange rates and also with floating rates.

4. Use IS-LM-BP analysis to discuss the effects of an increase in the money supply with complete sterilization of all payments imbalances.

5. Use IS-LM-BP analysis to derive the aggregate demand curve.

17. Review Questions

1. What are the four basic assumptions of the simple Keynesian model of an open economy? Describe the consequences of relaxing each assumption.

2. Discuss the importance of the degree of international capital mobility for the conduct of monetary and fiscal policy in an open economy.

3. Describe the macroeconomic performance of the U.S. economy during the 1980s in terms of the theory developed in this chapter.

4. Describe two distinct views of the role of the exchange rate in a floating rate system. Why does it matter whether one view or the other is correct? Is there any empirical evidence?

PART FOUR

Further Applications of International Monetary Theory

CHAPTER 10 International Macroeconomic Policy

1. Policy Dilemmas

Basic Ideas

1. The authorities cannot independently control the level of income and the trade balance, if expenditure policy is the only available tool.

2. A second tool, such as the exchange rate, allows both targets to be attained, in principle. A combination of the exchange rate and expenditure policy can be found that will just attain both types of balance at once.

3. With a fixed exchange rate, expenditure policy influences foreign aggregate demand in the same direction as domestic aggregate demand. Thus if countries use expenditure policy for internal balance, their individual efforts will reinforce each other when the economies are in phase, but will breed international conflict when they are out of phase.

4. If expenditure policies are used for internal balance, and the exchange rate is allowed to adjust to achieve external balance, countries will not find themselves in conflict if the degree of international capital mobility is low.

5. If fiscal policy is used for internal balance and capital is highly mobile, countries will likely find themselves in conflict.

6. Exchange rate variations influence foreign aggregate demand in the opposite direction from domestic aggregate demand. Thus if countries try to use the exchange rate for internal balance, their individual efforts will reinforce each other when the economies are out of phase, but will breed international conflict when they are in phase.

7. If the exchange rate is regarded as a policy target, rather than an instrument, we are again in the situation of trying to attain internal and external balance with fiscal and monetary policies.

1. Multiple choice: under which of the following circumstances would expenditure policy aimed at internal balance cause more international conflict with floating rates than with fixed rates?

1.1. No international capital mobility.

1.2. When monetary policy is the instrument and capital mobility is high.

1.3. When fiscal policy is the instrument and capital mobility is low.

1.4. When fiscal policy is the instrument and capital mobility is high.

1.5. None of the above.

2. Suppose that Italy has a *MPS* of one-sixth and a *MPM* of one-third. What increase in Italian autonomous spending would produce the same effect on foreign aggregate demand as would an increase of 100 in foreign autonomous spending?

Solution to Problem from the Text

10.0 *Suppose that inflation in each country is related to the level of aggregate demand, as discussed in section 7 of chapter 9 of the textbook. How does this modify the discussion in this section of the text?*

In this case the *OT* line, in Figure 10.1 in the textbook shows the only combinations of aggregate demands in the two countries for which a continuous adjustment of the exchange rate between those countries would not be ultimately required.

Additional Problems

1. Discuss possible policy conflicts between countries if the authorities in each country are concerned about external balance.

2. What are "beggar-my-neighbor" policies?

Answers to Self-Test

1. 1.4.

2. 150.

2. The Bretton Woods System

Basic Ideas

1. A new international monetary system was designed by the United Nations states toward the close of the Second World War.

2. The International Monetary Fund and the World Bank (IBRD) were established as institutional components of the new system.

3. The system was to feature an adjustable peg exchange rate arrangement and the free convertibility of national currencies for the purpose of current-account transactions.

4. Quota subscriptions of member states supply resources for the IMF, which uses them to make various loans, both conditional and unconditional, to members.

5. The Bretton Woods system was an example of a gold exchange standard, with the United States obligated to exchange gold for dollars at a fixed price with foreign central banks, and the latter obligated to peg their currencies to the U.S. dollar. As a result the dollar is an intervention and reserve currency.

6. The Special Drawing Right is an international reserve asset created by the IMF.

7. You should understand: **The mechanics of IMF functions, the basic outline of the Bretton Woods System, the nature of and reasons for the special role of the dollar, what SDRs are and how they are used.**

Self-Test

1. What does each of the following stand for: IMF, IBRD, SDR?

2. True or false: The "reserve tranche" is a quantity of funds the IMF keeps as a reserve to lend to countries should a global crisis seem imminent.

3. List the types of international reserve assets under the Bretton Woods system.

Solutions to Problems from the Text

10.1 *On December 30, 1986, the dollar exchange rate of the German mark was $.51, of the French franc was $.15, of the Japanese yen was $.006, of the pound sterling was $1.47, and of the Italian lira was $.0007. What was the price of one SDR in terms of U.S. dollars? In terms of French francs? In terms of Italian lire?*

SDR 1 = $1.1785 = fr7.8569 = 1683.6 lire.

10.2 *Until the creation of SDRs, there were three international reserve assets under the Bretton Woods system. The rapid growth of the world economy and of the volume of international transactions during the years that this system existed certainly made for a substantial increase in the world's need for international reserves. How reasonable do you think it would have been*

*to expect this increased need to actually have been met by
increases in each of the three reserve assets?*

Increases in gold could have been expected to be modest at best, since
they could come about only through new mining or by enticing some
out of private hoards, both unlikely with a fixed gold price. Increases
in aggregate reserve tranche positions could have been accomplished
by IMF quota increases, but these would entail a corresponding
reduction in other reserve assets. Increases in reserve currency holdings
were the most likely.

10.3 *In view of the intervention obligations of the Bretton Woods
system, what was the maximum percentage by which the market
value of the dollar could fluctuate relative to any other
currency? What was the maximum percentage by which any two
(nondollar) currencies could fluctuate relative to each other?*

With all (nondollar) currencies restricted to be within 1 percent of
their dollar pegs, the exchange rate of the dollar in terms of any other
currency could vary within a 2 percent band, whereas the exchange rate
of any two nondollar currencies could vary within a 4 percent band.

Additional Problems

1. Answer Problem 10.1 above with recent values of the relevant
   exchange rates. Compare your answers with the actual values of the
   SDR (see Appendix II of the textbook for data sources).

2. What do you think is the role of the IMF in dealing with the recent
   debt problems of many LDCs?

Answers to Self-Test

1. International Monetary Fund, International Bank for Reconstruction
   and Development, Special Drawing Right.

2. False.

3. Gold, reserve currencies, unconditional borrowing rights at the IMF,
   SDRs.

3. The Bretton Woods System in Operation

Basic Ideas

1. The Bretton Woods system went into operation in the late 1940s,
   though it wasn't until 1959 that most industrial countries had
   accepted the convertibility obligation, and the majority of LDCs still
   have not.

2. The early years were characterized by "dollar scarcity," the 1960s by "dollar glut."

3. There was a series of steadily worsening balance of payments crises during the 1960s.

4. Be sure you understand: **the confidence problem, the nature of the debate surrounding the asymmetric position of the dollar, the problems involved in maintaining an adjustable peg in the face of national autonomy and a high degree of international capital mobility.**

Self-Test

1. Who are in the "Group of Ten"?

2. Multiple choice: The "confidence problem" is that:
   2.1. It is unrealistic to expect private markets to maintain confidence in currencies not linked to gold, but impossible for all currencies to be linked to just one metal.
   2.2. The United States must run deficits to satisfy the world need for dollar reserves, but those deficits undermine world confidence in the value of the dollar as a reserve asset.
   2.3. The Arabs could not have been expected, in the early 1970s, to have much confidence in the currencies of countries dependent upon them, but there was nowhere else they could have turned for a store of value for their newfound wealth.
   2.4. All of the above.
   2.5. None of the above.

3. True or false: The U.S. government thought that the reserve currency status of the dollar was an unmixed blessing.

Solutions to Problems from the Text

10.4 *Discuss how each of the following might be interpreted as evidence in the debate over whether U.S. payments deficits were supply-determined (due to a failure of the United States to adopt measures to eliminate its deficit) or demand-determined (due to the failure of foreign countries to eliminate their surpluses):*

   a. *The United States improved its current-account position in the early and mid-1960s, but the overall payments deficits continued.*

   b. *Even as the IMF was allocating a new reserve asset, in the early 1970s, the American deficit exploded.*

   a. Demand determined.

   b. Supply determined.

10.5 *The text discussed the role of speculative capital movements with an adjustable peg. How would this discussion change in the presence of each of the following alternative exchange regimes: free floating, managed floating, fixed exchange rates.*

The problems discussed in the text would be absent with free floating, since the authorities would not stake out a position to be defended at all costs (or at any costs, for that matter), and with fixed rates, where there would be no possibility of an exchange rate change in any case. With managed floating, it would depend on the way in which the authorities managed their float.

Answers to Self-Test

1. The United States, Canada, Britain, Japan, Sweden, France, Germany, Italy, Belgium, the Netherlands, and (the eleventh member) Switzerland.

2. 2.2.

3. False.

4. Collapse of the Bretton Woods System and After

Basic Ideas

1. With huge U.S. deficits, the Bretton Woods system collapsed in the early 1970s: industrial countries abandoned their obligations to peg to the dollar and the United States renounced its obligation to sell gold to foreign central banks for dollars.

2. Attempts consciously to design a new international monetary system —or to redesign the old system—came to nought.

3. As a result we now have a hybrid system. Most industrial countries have managed floats, with the notable exception of the EMS. Most LDCs peg their currencies, either to the dollar or some other major currency or else to a basket of currencies or to the SDR.

Solution to Problem from the Text

10.6 *The Smithsonian negotiations included considerable debate over whether the depreciation of the dollar should involve a dollar devaluation or just the revaluation of other currencies. Can you think of any reasons for this, since everyone knew that the United States would not restore official gold convertibility in any case?*

For reasons of national pride mainly. But, there were some outstanding contracts and international agreements and obligations expressed in terms of gold. The values of these in terms of national

currencies were sensitive to the exact combination of dollar
devaluation and revaluation of other currencies adopted.

Additional Problems

1. Give a narrative of the major events in the three years leading up to
   the collapse of the Bretton Woods system in 1973.

2. Describe the Committee of 20, the Rambouillet meeting, the Jamaica
   Agreement, and the Second Amendment to the IMF Articles of
   Agreement.

5. International Monetary Reform Issues

Basic Ideas

1. Debate over reform of the international monetary system has centered
   on reserve assets and the nature of the exchange-rate regime.

2. Gold has become an inactive reserve asset, currencies can no longer be
   pegged to it, and the IMF is attempting to replace it with the SDR.

3. It has been proposed that the IMF establish a substitution account to
   trade SDRs to central banks for their dollar holdings. But agreement
   has not been reached on this.

4. It has also been proposed that intervention be done with a number of
   currencies, rather than with just dollars.

5. There have been many proposals for regulating, mandating, or
   otherwise restricting national intervention in the exchange markets,
   but nothing has been done.

6. There have been isolated instances of coordinated intervention by
   several central banks.

7. Be sure you know about: **the dollar overhang, the substitution
   account, multicurrency intervention, the IMF Guidelines,
   and Decision on Surveillance.**

Solutions to Problems from the Text

10.7 *Under what circumstances could the existence of a substitution
     account lessen the asymmetric position of the United States?*

By itself, the establishment of a substitution account would not alter
intervention practices. Also, if the IMF held its dollars in interest
earning form (a matter for negotiation during the establishment of
such an account) and if the IMF were neither more nor less willing to
accumulate dollars than central banks had been (or if the latter were
neither more nor less willing to accumulate additional dollars than

they had been before the account) the U.S. position would be no different.

10.9 *Suppose that the fluctuations of some exchange rates consist of random deviations from a constant equilibrium value. If a central bank then undertakes to lean against the wind, would its intervention on balance serve to move the exchange rate toward equilibrium or away from it? Answer the same question if the exchange rate fluctuations instead consist of random deviations from a moving equilibrium.*

Leaning against the wind could be expected, on balance, to move an exchange rate neither closer to nor further from a constant equilibrium, but further from a moving one.

Additional Problem

Discuss the likely consequences of a unilateral U.S. return to the gold standard, under the assumption that other major countries do not follow suit and that the IMF's rules and policies are not altered.

6. Review Questions

1. Describe the basic features of the Bretton Woods system.

2. Analyze the Bretton Woods system in the light of section 1's discussion of policy dilemmas.

3. Describe the basic features of the present international monetary system.

4. Analyze the present international monetary system in the light of section 1's discussion of policy dilemmas.

CHAPTER 11   International Financial Markets

1. The Foreign Exchange Market

Basic Ideas

1. The currencies of different countries are exchanged for each other on the foreign exchange market.

2. At the retail end, firms and individuals with foreign business transactions can buy or sell foreign exchange, for domestic currency, with their bankers.

3. In order to be able to service their customers, the international departments of large banks participate in the interbank market for foreign exchange.

4. There are such participating banks in the major financial centers of the world. These banks deal with other banks in the same center (usually through a broker) or with banks in foreign centers (with some of whom they are connected by direct telephone or telex lines).

5. Arbitrage keeps the exchange rates of different currency pairs in different centers mutually consistent.

6. The U.S. dollar is especially important because it is often a vehicle currency, a central-bank intervention currency, and an international unit of account.

7. In most foreign centers the most important foreign exchange transactions are those involving the local currency and the U.S. dollar, and New York is often an important alternative center for such transactions.

8. Points to understand: **Figure 11.2 in the textbook, triangular arbitrage, vehicle currency, intervention currency.**

Self-Test

1. On the basis of the data in Table 11.1 in the textbook what should be the price of the Dutch guilder in terms of the French franc?

2. True or false: If the New York foreign exchange market were officially abolished, the international trade of the United States would disappear, eventually, if not at once.

Solutions to Problems from the Text

11.1 *Figures 11.1 and 11.2 in the textbook assumed that contracts were in terms of the currency of the exporter. How are the figures changed if contracts are in the importer's currency? If all contracts are in dollars?*

If contracts are in the importer's currency, Acme Spirits pays $20,000 for the whiskey to the Scottish distillery, which instead (of Acme) sells the $20,000 to Bank A for pounds. Similarly, Coagulated Mush pays pounds to the American agricultural exporter, who then sells them to Bank B for dollars. Other transactions remain the same.

11.2 *In Figure 11.2 in the textbook trade between the United States and the United Kingdom was assumed to be in balance. Suppose instead that, at the same prices, Acme Spirits imports 400 cases of whiskey, soybean exports remaining equal to 4,000 bushels. How is the figure changed? Discuss various possible consequences, using the theory of chapters 7, 8 and 9 of the text.*

In this case Acme Spirits must pay $40,000 to the banking system for 20,000 pounds to pay for the whiskey, the other transactions remaining the same. Thus there is an excess supply of $20,000 in the world and an excess demand of 10,000 pounds. These can be met by a depreciation of the dollar relative to the pound or by central-bank intervention and the consequent payments imbalances; this was discussed in chapters 7 and 8.

11.3 *The foreign exchange market described in this section of the textbook involves bank deposits. But exchanges of currencies also take place, though on a very much smaller scale. For example, a tourist might buy a few pound notes from her New York bank before leaving for London, and she might sell a few pound notes to that bank when she returns. Describe the influence of arbitrage on the relation between the dollar price of pound notes in New York and the pound price of dollars in London. How do you think this influence compares with that of arbitrage in the foreign exchange market as discussed in the textbook?*

The significant cost of actually transporting currency from country to country prevents arbitrage from equalizing exchange rates for notes around the world as closely as rates for bank deposits.

Additional Problem

Find out, from your local bank, the current buying and selling prices for small quantities of U.K. currency. Compare these prices with the current exchange rate for the U.K. pound, as quoted in the financial pages of your newspaper.

Answers to Self-Test

1. 2.9495 French francs per guilder (on Fri.).

2. False.

2. The Forward Market

Basic Ideas

1. The forward exchange market is one in which individuals agree today to exchange, at some specific date in the future, a certain amount of one currency for a certain amount of another currency.

2. Firms and individuals can use the forward exchange market to protect themselves against the risk of future exchange rate fluctuations.

3. One explanation of the relation between the spot and forward exchange rates is that of covered interest parity: the forward premium on foreign exchange must equal the interest differential.

4. Another explanation of the relation between the spot and forward exchange rates involves speculation: the forward premium must equal the expected rate of appreciation of the spot rate.

5. The two explanations are consistent in the sense that a high degree of capital mobility will cause the interest differential to equal the expected rate of appreciation of the spot rate.

6. Items to understand: **covered interest arbitrage and covered interest parity; how forward exchange allows international trade to proceed unimpeded by exchange risk; the potential consistency of the two explanations of the relation between spot and forward exchange rates.**

Self-Test

1. True or false: Interest arbitrageurs will buy forward exchange if the forward premium exceeds the interest differential of domestic interest rates relative to foreign rates.

2. True or false: Speculators will buy forward exchange if the forward premium exceeds the expected appreciation of the spot rate.

Solutions to Problems from the Text

11.5 *In the textbook, Acme Spirits covered itself against exchange risk by buying pounds forward. Another way of accomplishing this would be to borrow dollars from its bank, use the dollars to buy spot pounds, and deposit the pounds in a British bank until the time came to pay for the whiskey. What would be the cost of this second method? Which method would probably be cheaper and why?*

If R denotes the spot price of pounds and i_{US} and i_{UK} the relevant U.S. and U.K. interest rates, the total dollar cost of the second method would be:

$$\frac{R(1 + i_{US})}{(1 + i_{UK})}.$$

11.6 *Suppose that the U.S. interest rate is 8 percent per annum, the U.K. rate is 12 percent per annum, the spot price of a pound is $2.06, and the one-year forward price is $2.00. Describe the interest arbitrage this should induce.*

$$1 + i_{US} = 1.08 < (1 + i_{UK})\left(\frac{R_F}{R_S}\right) = (1.12)\left(\frac{2}{2.06}\right) = 1.09$$

so arbitrageurs sell U.S. Treasury bills, buy pounds spot, buy U.K. Treasury bills, and sell pounds forward.

11.7 *Suppose in Problem 11.6 that the 90-day forward price of a pound is $2.02. Describe the interest arbitrage that should be induced.*

The 90-day interest rate equals one-fourth of the per annum rate. Thus $1 + i_{US} = 1.02 > (1 + i_{UK})(R_F/R_S) = (1.03)(2.02/2.06) = 1.01$ so arbitrage is in the opposite direction to that in Problem 11.6.

11.8 *Can you think of any reason why capital movements should be less than perfect if traders are free to buy and sell spot and forward foreign exchange and the treasury bills of all countries?*

Forward cover can remove exchange risk, but there are other risks involved in investing in foreign treasury bills that are not present when investing in domestic treasury bills. The forward exchange contract is an obligation of a commercial bank, whereas treasury bills are obligations of national governments. Also there is a chance that exchange controls could be imposed before the foreign bills mature, making it impossible (or expensive) to repatriate funds. For these reasons, a bank may prefer to invest in the treasury bills of its own government, even when covered interest arbitrage promises a profit.

*11.10 *In chapter 9 of the textbook we showed that exchange depreciation causes domestic inflation. Suppose Acme Spirits were confident that, should the dollar depreciate relative to the pound, the American price of scotch whiskey would quickly rise in the same proportion. How should this influence the firm's decision on obtaining forward cover for its obligations to the U.K. distillery? What if Acme Spirits knew that dollar depreciation would raise the U.S. price of the whiskey, but was unsure about how much or how soon?*

If Acme Spirits knew that the American price of scotch whiskey would quickly rise in the same proportion as any depreciation of the dollar relative to the pound, the company would incur no risk from dealing in pound denominated contracts for its whiskey imports: whatever it lost on buying the whiskey, as a result of a dollar depreciation, would be made up when it sold the whiskey domestically. Thus Acme Spirits would not enter the forward market to protect itself. If the firm were unsure about how much of a dollar depreciation would be translated into a higher domestic price, or about how soon it would occur, the firm would still be subject to exchange risk and so it would obtain some forward cover. But it would not cover completely, since the domestic price changes would still offer some protection.

*11.11 *Between 1973 and 1979 many controls on international capital movements were removed by the United Kingdom and Germany. Can you discern any effects of this in Tables 11.7 and 11.8 in the textbook? Explain.*

The failure of interest parity to hold in 1973, as revealed in Table 11.7 in the textbook, was due in good part to existing exchange controls and the threat of future controls. These were largely absent in 1979.

Additional Problems

1. Using the data in Table 11.1 in the textbook, calculate the difference between the U.S. and British 60-day interest rates that would have to have held on March 2, 1987, in order to maintain covered interest parity.

2. Using the data in Table 11.1 in the textbook, calculate the difference between the Canadian and British 60-day interest rates that would have to have held on March 2, 1987, in order to maintain covered interest parity.

3. Work out the interest-arbitrage argument in the textbook if instead the trader is British and is concerned about the value of his assets in pounds rather than in dollars. Do the same for the speculation example in the textbook.

4. Using the data in Table 11.1 in the textbook, calculate the expected appreciation of the Canadian dollar in terms of the British pound for the ninety days following March 2, 1987, according to the speculation theory of the forward premium.

Answers to Self-Test

1. False.

2. False.

*3. Exploring Further: Equilibrium in the Forward Exchange Market

Basic Ideas

1. The *arbitrage schedule* records the demand for forward exchange—for the purpose of covered interest arbitrage—that would be forthcoming at each value of the forward premium.

2. With perfect capital mobility, the arbitrage schedule is infinitely elastic at the value of the forward premium equal to the interest differential. But transactions cost, exchange risk, and default risk can prevent capital mobility from being perfect.

3. The *speculation schedule* records the supply of forward exchange—for the purpose of speculation—that would be forthcoming at each value of the forward premium.

4. The speculation schedule is infinitely elastic at the value of the forward premium equal to the expected value of the spot rate, if that expectation is held with complete certainty or if speculators are indifferent toward risk.

5. The intersection of the arbitrage and speculation schedules shows the equilibrium forward premium, where the net demand for forward exchange for interest arbitrage just equals the net supply offered by speculators.

6. If the interest differential and the expected appreciation of the spot rate are unequal, the forward premium will lie somewhere between the two.

7. A high degree of international capital mobility will put pressure on the interest differential and the expected spot appreciation to coincide, and to thereby equal the forward premium as well.

Solutions to Problems from the Text

11.12 *Show graphically how the forward exchange market would likely react to each of the following events, and describe the consequences in words.*

   a. *An increase in domestic interest rates.*

   b. *An increase in the expected future spot rate.*

   c. *An increased fear that foreign banks may be unable or unwilling to honor their forward commitments.*

   Relate this to the situations described in Table 11.8 in the textbook.

   a. An increase in domestic interest rates would shift the arbitrage schedule up, so that equilibrium would move up along the speculation schedule.

b. An increase in the expected future spot rate would shift the speculator's supply schedule up, so that equilibrium would move along the arbitrage schedule.

c. Both schedules would become more inelastic.

11.13 *The text assumed that commodity trade between the United States and the United Kingdom was balanced. How would the analysis change if instead the United States had a large trade surplus with the United Kingdom?*

If merchants obtained forward cover, the large U.S. trade surplus would imply a large net supply of forward pounds by merchants. Thus equilibrium would not occur where the arbitrage and speculation schedules intersect, but rather at a forward premium for which the excess demand for forward pounds of arbitrageurs and speculators equaled the excess supply of merchants.

11.14 *Show geometrically the result of intervention by the Bank of England to support the spot exchange rate of the pound relative to the dollar. Do the same for intervention to support the forward rate.*

Intervention to support the spot pound would shift the speculation schedule down. Support of the forward rate, to be successful, would require the authorities to make up the difference between the speculation and arbitrage schedules at the forward premium corresponding to the forward rate being supported.

Additional Problems

1. How would the diagrams of this section be affected if people suddenly thought that there was a very good chance that the U.K. authorities would prevent banks from honoring their commitments to buy sterling, but that there was very little chance of any other controls being established?

2. What would happen if the authorities in the two countries decided to intervene in the spot and forward markets so as to maintain permanently a forward premium on the domestic currency that exceeded the expected appreciation of the spot rate?

4. Foreign Currency Futures and Options

Basic Ideas

1. A purchaser of a foreign currency futures contract pays now in exchange for a certain amount of a foreign currency at a certain date in the future.

2. Foreign currency futures are standardized contracts traded on organized and regulated exchanges.

3. Purchasers of foreign currency futures typically put up only a margin and close out their positions before actually taking delivery.

4. A foreign currency option gives the purchaser the right to buy (*call option*) or to sell (*put option*) a certain amount of a certain currency at a certain price for a certain time.

Self-Test

1. What is the "strike price" in an option contract? How is it related to the price of the option?

2. What combination of options transactions is equivalent to buying £100,000 ninety days forward at the forward price of $1.60/£?

Answers to Self-Test

1. The price at which an option can be exercised. A higher strike price reduces the price of a call option but increases the price of a put option. Be sure you can deduce why.

2. Write a European style put option for £100,000 with a strike price of $1.60/£, and buy a European style call option for £100,000 at a strike price of $1.60/£. If the spot price turns out to be below $1.60/£, the put option will be exercised by its buyer; if the spot price is above this, you will exercise the call option.

5. The Eurodollar Market

Basic Ideas

1. Eurodollars are U.S. dollars on deposit outside the United States.

2. The Eurodollar market has grown from virtually nothing in the 1950s to over a trillion dollars in size today. There are also large markets in several other Eurocurrencies.

3. Foreign banks in the Eurodollar market accept dollar deposits and make dollar-denominated loans. These deposits are "backed up" by dollars on deposit in the United States.

4. Some dollar depositors, such as the Soviet Union and some Arab governments, use the Eurodollar market because they wish to deal in dollars without exposing themselves to the jurisdiction of the United States.

5. The Eurodollar market is unregulated and thus free of legal reserve requirements and controls on interest rates. This has given it a competitive advantage, which at times has been substantial, over national money markets.

6. Be sure you understand: **Eurocurrency mechanics; the meaning of Eurodollar, Eurocurrency, Eurobank.**

Self-Test

1. Multiple choice: Eurodollars are:
   1.1. Dollars issued by European central banks.
   1.2. Dollars owned by European central banks.
   1.3. Foreign currencies owned by Americans.
   1.4. Deposits in American banks by foreigners.
   1.5. None of the above.

2. True or false: The U.S. money supply increases when an American resident borrows Eurodollars from a London bank.

Solutions to Problems from the Text

11.15 *Suppose that Bayer acquires $5 million drawn on an American bank and deposits it in the London branch of Chase Manhattan. Chase's New York office then borrows $4 million from its London branch. Show the balance sheet entries of both the home office and the branch. What are the effects on the sizes of the Eurodollar market and the U.S. and U.K. money supplies?*

New York		London	
Reserves:	Demand Deposits:	Reserves: $1 million (deposit in some U.S. bank)	Demand Deposits: $5 million
$4 million	$4 million	Loans: $4 million	

The Eurodollar market increases by $5 million; there is no effect on either money supply.

11.16 *The text showed that U.S. reserve requirements gave Eurobanks a competitive edge over domestic banks. But Eurodollars are mostly time deposits, and U.S. reserve requirements for time deposits are quite low, whereas the requirements for demand deposits are much higher. Would you not therefore expect Eurodollars to consist mainly of demand deposits? Why do you think this has not happened?*

Many Eurodollar time deposits are simply overnight, and many more are a week or less. These are basically the same as demand deposits.

11.17 *The Depository Institutions Deregulation and Monetary Control Act phased out all U.S. ceilings on deposit interest rates by 1986. What do you think were the effects on the Eurocurrency markets?*

Deregulation eliminated the competitive advantage the Euromarkets enjoyed because of interest rate ceilings, but they still have an advantage because of reserve requirements. The interest rate ceilings were particularly important in the past when monetary conditions in the United States became very tight; thus deregulation will help prevent such tight money episodes from accelerating the growth of the Eurodollar market. But that market is by now sufficiently well developed so that it does not need a competitive advantage to survive.

11.18 *Measure what happens to (1) U.S. liabilities to foreign official institutions, (2) German official holdings of dollars, and (3) the size of the Eurodollar market in the following series of transactions:*

a. *The Bundesbank switches $1 billion from its account at Morgan Guaranty New York to Morgan Guaranty London (MGL) in order to obtain a higher interest rate.*

b. *MGL lends $900 million to a German firm (which is facing tight monetary conditions inside Germany). The German firm in turn sells the dollars to the Bundesbank for marks in order to invest in Germany. The Bundesbank deposits the $900 million at MGL.*

c. *Another German firm borrows $810 million from MGL and trades the dollars for marks. In turn the Bundesbank deposits the $810 million at MGL.*

d. *The Bundesbank lodges a protest with the Federal Reserve Board complaining that it is impossible to maintain an anti-inflationary policy so long as the United States is flooding Europe with excess dollars. How should the Fed reply?*

a. The Eurodollar market increases by $1 billion.

b. The Eurodollar market, U.S. liabilities to foreign official institutions, and German official dollar holdings increase by $900 million.

c. U.S. liabilities to foreign official institutions and German official dollar holdings increase by $810 million.

d. The Fed could urge the Bundesbank not to deposit its dollars in the Eurodollar market. The latter would perhaps reply that it wouldn't matter if they were deposited in New York instead.

*11.19 *Suppose that Texaco and British Petroleum each make $500 million payments to the government of Kuwait:*

a. *Texaco makes payment by issuing a draft on its account with City Bank/New York (CBNY);*

b. BP sells spot sterling for dollars causing the Bank of England to draw down its dollar reserves held with CBNY by $500 million in order to support the spot rate;

c. Kuwait deposits the $1 billion with CB London.

Show how these transactions affect:

i. The U.S. and U.K. money supplies;

ii. The size of the Eurodollar market.

In what way would these transactions tend to influence interest rates in the United States, the United Kingdom, and the Eurodollar market? How might this alter patterns of borrowing and lending?

The Bank of England's intervention has increased the U.S. money supply and reduced the U.K. money supply by $500 million (ignoring any subsequent sterilization); the Kuwaiti deposit has increased the Eurodollar market by $1 billion. This should reduce interest rates in the United States and in the Eurodollar market, and increase them in the United Kingdom.

*11.20 During the mid-1960s many observers worried that the Eurodollar system would collapse in the face of widespread speculation against the dollar. Since that time we have witnessed several speculative episodes, and in each instance not only has the Eurodollar market survived, but it has actually increased in size. Explain why this should have been expected by analyzing the impact of the expectation of a dollar depreciation on:

a. Nonbank demand for Eurodollar borrowing;

b. Non(commercial) bank supply of Eurodollar deposits.

Other things being equal, nonbank demand for Eurodollar borrowing could have been expected to rise, with the borrowers expecting to repay their loans with depreciated dollars. Those who had to hold dollars (such as central banks) would also have been more likely to deposit them in the Euromarkets, where the unregulated interest rates would be free to rise in anticipation of a dollar depreciation.

Additional Problem

Investigate current activity in the Eurocurrency markets (see Appendix II of the textbook for data sources). Interpret in the light of the discussion in this section of the text.

Answers to Self-Test

1. 1.5.

2. False.

6. Should the Eurocurrency Markets Be Regulated?

Basic Ideas

1. It is frequently argued that the Eurocurrency markets should be regulated because:

   a. They have caused a huge increase in the global money supply.

   b. They prevent individual countries from controlling their own money supplies.

   c. They allow deficit countries to borrow indefinitely and thus postpone painful adjustments until it is too late.

   d. They furnish a large volume of liquid funds that can be easily moved around, causing global disruption of exchange and interest rates.

   e. They are unregulated and so could collapse after a speculative bubble, bringing on a worldwide panic.

2. Many of the alleged problems have to do with international capital mobility, of which the Eurocurrency markets are more a symptom than a cause.

3. Regulation is very difficult in any case, because the Eurodollar market will simply move from any place where regulations are imposed to some other place where they are not.

Self-Test

1. What does "IBF" stand for and what is it?

2. What is the Eurodollar multiplier if Eurobanks normally keep 2 percent of their dollar deposits as reserves, and if about 22 percent of all Eurodollar loans end up redeposited in the Eurodollar market?

Solution to Problem from the Text

11.21 *Describe the Eurodollar carousel in terms of the discussion of sterilization and offset in chapter 8 of the textbook. Should the decision by the central banks, to deposit no additional reserves in the Eurodollar market, actually have made their job any easier, assuming they wanted to intervene and sterilize? Why?*

Assuming the central banks would both intervene and sterilize in either case, the decision not to deposit additional reserves in the Eurodollar market simply meant that they were deposited in New York instead, so that the global total of dollar deposits was unchanged. Further, if the central banks' substitution of New York deposits for Eurodollar deposits induced an offsetting shift by private borrowers, there would be no effect on the distribution of those global deposits either. The only effect, in this latter case, would have been that the identity of New York depositors would have shifted towards foreign central banks and away from other types of depositors (this could have had a slight effect to the extent that New York reserve requirements for deposits of foreign official institutions differ, on the one hand, from the requirements that otherwise apply in New York, and, on the other hand, from practices in the Eurodollar market).

Answers to Self-Test

1. International Banking Facility.

2. 1.25.

7. The Efficiency of the Foreign Exchange Markets

Basic Ideas

1. A market is efficient if its prices fully reflect all currently available information.

2. Market efficiency is important because economic agents base their actions on the prices they face.

3. Covered interest parity is an aspect of exchange market efficiency, since the parity relationship holds when the spot and forward exchange rates reflect the available information about interest rates.

4. Covered interest parity holds almost exactly in the Eurocurrency markets, and normally comes reasonably close to holding between national money markets as well.

5. The forward premium is often an inaccurate predictor of future spot appreciation. But it comes close to being an unbiased predictor, and is nearly as good as any other predictor. Recent evidence does indicate, though, that the forward premium is not in fact exactly unbiased. This could reflect a risk premium necessary to induce people to hold certain currencies.

6. Be sure you understand: **market efficiency, why it matters, risk premium, joint hypothesis.**

Self-Test

1. Multiple choice: Which of the following is an indicator of efficiency in the foreign exchange market:
   1.1. High commissions.
   1.2. Low commissions.
   1.3. The fact that spot deliveries occur within two business days.
   1.4. The ability to obtain forward cover for any date in the future.
   1.5. None of the above.

2. True or false: A foreign currency pays a risk premium when its forward rate exceeds the spot exchange rate.

3. True or false: If the forward rate is an unbiased predictor of the future spot rate, a speculator betting consistently against the former would almost certainly end up losing money, even though he could make large gains on occasion.

Solution to Problem from the Text

11.22 *German exchange controls on capital inflows were relaxed on January 30, 1974, but Figure 11.7 in the textbook shows that the Euromark and German interbank interest rates actually moved together a few months* earlier. *Can you think of any reason for this?*

Individuals anticipated in advance that exchange controls were about to be relaxed.

Answers to Self-Test

1. 1.5.

2. False.

3. True.

8. International Credit Markets

Basic Ideas

1. Foreign bonds are bonds issued in the domestic bond market by foreign entities.

2. Many foreign bonds are issued in Switzerland. Other important centers include the United States, Germany, and Japan.

3. Eurobonds are denominated in a currency, or a combination of currencies, other than that of the country in which they are issued.

Self-Test

1. Multiple choice: Most Eurobonds are denominated in:
   1.1. U.S. dollars.
   1.2. Yen.
   1.3. Swiss francs.
   1.4. Currency cocktails.
   1.5. None of the above.

2. Are Eurobonds typically bearer bonds or registered bonds?

Answers to Self-Test

1. 1.1.

2. Bearer bonds.

9. Review Questions

1. Describe the basic international financial markets.

2. What do we mean by the *efficiency* of the foreign exchange markets?
   Describe relevant evidence.

3. Explain how spot and forward foreign exchange rates are related to
   each other.

PART FIVE

The Modern World Economy

CHAPTER 12   Economic Integration

1. The Basic Theory of Biased Integration

Basic Ideas

1. This section discusses reductions in barriers to trade or to factor mobility, or a unification of economic policies, between a group of countries.

2. A reduction in trade barriers between a group of countries causes *trade creation* between them.

3. The fact that each of these countries now discriminates in favor of its partners, relative to those countries that are not parties to the agreement, produces *trade diversion.*

4. *Trade modification* results when a group of countries reduce their tariffs in a nondiscriminatory fashion, but the reductions take place on goods that are largely traded within the group.

5. Mutual tariff reductions can alter the terms of trade between the partners, and also the terms of trade of the partners with the rest of the world.

6. Integration can allow the partners to enjoy the benefits of international scale economies and increased product differentiation.

7. Attempts of countries to integrate macroeconomic policies often focus on first maintaining fixed exchange rates relative to each other.

Self-Test

1. Multiple choice: Britain joins the Common Market and imports wheat from France rather than from Canada and the United States. This is an example of:
   - 1.1. Trade creation.
   - 1.2. Trade diversion.
   - 1.3. Trade modification.
   - 1.4. All of the above.
   - 1.5. None of the above.

2. Multiple choice: Britain joins the Common Market and begins importing wine from France in exchange for beer. This is an example of:
   - 2.1. Trade creation.

2.2. Trade diversion.
2.3. Trade modification.
2.4. All of the above.
2.5. None of the above.

3. Multiple choice: Britain joins the Common Market and reduces imports of tea from India because the British are now drinking wine from France instead of tea. This is an example of:
   3.1. Trade creation.
   3.2. Trade diversion.
   3.3. Trade modification.
   3.4. All of the above.
   3.5. None of the above.

4. True or false: The formation of the EEC was followed not by an increase in inter-industry trade and specialization, but rather by an increase in intra-industry trade and a consequent reduction in specialization.

Solutions to Problems from the Text

12.2 *Should the existence of the guest-worker system discussed in chapter 6 of the textbook prove a help or a hindrance in the effort of the EEC to achieve monetary integration?*

If the guest-worker systems of the various EEC countries are in fact stabilizing aggregate demand in those countries, as they are intended in part to do, this should help the cause of monetary integration, because it would reduce the tendency for the individual EEC countries to pursue divergent macroeconomic policies.

12.3 *Suppose the world is as described in the Heckscher-Ohlin-Samuelson model of chapter 3 of the textbook, except that there are several countries instead of just two. Is integration more likely to be beneficial to two countries if their relative endowments are similar or if they are different?*

Greater differences in relative endowments could be expected to accentuate both trade creation and trade diversion.

12.4 *Are those gains from integration that are due to international scale economies and product differentiation more likely to be large if the partners are similar or if they are different?*

If they are similar.

*12.5 *Suppose that F and G mutually eliminate tariffs on each other's products and then jointly levy an optimum common tariff on goods from R. Can you say anything about the significance of trade diversion?*

There would be no problem with trade diversion because F and G would be exploiting their position relative to R to the full. Any trade diversion that did occur would serve the purpose of helping to improve the partners' terms of trade with R.

Additional Problem

In terms of the concepts discussed in this section of the textbook, speculate about the consequences for the United States of the formation of the EEC.

Answers to Self-Test

1. 1.2.

2. 2.1.

3. 3.3.

4. True.

2. Biased Integration in Practice

Basic Ideas

1. There have been many attempts at economic integration since the Second World War. Two of these are of major historical significance.

2. The first of these is the large reduction on barriers to the trade of manufactures enacted by the DCs under GATT auspices.

3. The second is the economic integration that has taken place in Western Europe: the EEC and also its free trade arrangements with other Western European countries.

4. There have been many attempts at integration between LDCs, but they have had quite limited success so far.

5. Be sure you understand: **the distinctions between the major types of economic integration, the various attempts at integration.**

Self-Test

1. What do the following stand for: CAP, EFTA, LAFTA, ASEAN?

2. Multiple choice: a common market differs from a customs union in that:
   2.1. The countries in a common market agree to sell on equal terms to the rest of the world, but not necessarily to buy on equal terms, as is the case with a customs union.
   2.2. The countries in a common market agree to buy on equal terms from the rest of the world, but not necessarily to sell on equal terms, as is the case with a customs union.
   2.3. The customs union allows free factor mobility, as does a common market, but also free trade in goods.

2.4. The common market allows free trade in goods, as does a customs union, but also free factor mobility.

2.5. None of the above.

Solutions to Problems from the Text

12.6 *Why is it necessary for a customs union to negotiate some way of distributing the joint tariff revenues, rather than simply letting each country keep what it collects (hint: consider the geographical position of Luxembourg)?*

Formation of a customs union itself alters the distribution of tariff collections among countries.

12.8 *The United States strongly supported formation of the EEC. Why?*

Basically for noneconomic reasons.

12.9 *Discuss the implications of the GATT multilateral tariff reductions for the significance of the EEC.*

The abolition of internal EEC tariffs became much less significant.

Additional Problem

Can you think of any reasons why the European attempts at integration were notably more successful than LDC attempts?

Answers to Self-Test

1. Common Agricultural Policy, European Free Trade Association, Latin American Free Trade Association, Association of Southeast Asian Nations.

2. 2.4.

3. The International Trade of Centrally Planned Economies; East-West Trade

Basic Ideas

1. Since prices do not reflect opportunity costs in centrally planned economies, those economies cannot allow foreign residents freely to buy and sell there, or domestic residents to buy and sell freely abroad. That is, their currencies must be inconvertible.

2. The international trade of these countries is instead handled by foreign trade organizations.

3. Trade among communist countries is basically bilateral and uses prices derived from Western market prices.

4. Despite the political barriers, East-West trade has been growing relative to East-East trade. The former is in some ways easier, since it can use Western market prices directly.

Self-Test

1. What does COMECON stand for?

2. Multiple choice: Economic integration in Eastern Europe:
   2.1. Is a matter of course, since the Soviet Union calls all the shots anyway.
   2.2. Is complete, because those countries have no tariffs.
   2.3. Became a reality when, after the formation of COMECON, those countries integrated their planning procedures.
   2.4. All of the above.
   2.5. None of the above.

3. True or false: East-West trade is usually conducted with Western currencies.

Solutions to Problems from the Text

12.11 *Why does the Polish government go to the trouble of printing up and issuing bony to dollar depositors, instead of simply giving back the dollars that were deposited in the first place?*

So that the government can immediately spend the dollars abroad, or earn interest on them, without waiting for the dollars to be spent in the state stores.

12.12 *The Soviet grain purchases in 1972 raised world grain prices. What was the effect on the welfare of American urban dwellers, American farmers, and America as a whole? How was the welfare of each of these groups affected by the American policies followed at the time?*

Since the United States was a grain exporter, the increase in world grain prices, by itself, raised the welfare of America as a whole and of American farmers, but lowered the welfare of American urban dwellers (who are net buyers of grain). The effective increase in export subsidies, however, reduced the welfare of the country as a whole and further reduced that of urban dwellers.

12.13 *Assume that American efforts to persuade other countries not to increase grain sales to the Soviet Union failed. What would have been the effect of the American embargo if: (a) world grain supplies were plentiful and the agricultural programs of most grain-producing states were buying grain to keep up prices; (b) grain supplies were tight and agricultural programs were inactive? How would your answers change if U.S. persuasion had some success?*

With prices held up by support programs, the Soviet purchases would simply result in fewer government purchases and have no effect on market prices. Since the various government programs would isolate national markets from each other, the country in which the Soviets purchased the grain would benefit (since they could reduce their own government purchases by a like amount) and other countries would be unaffected. Thus the only effect of the embargo would be to benefit the country in which the Soviets instead bought their grain. With grain supplies tight and government programs inactive, the Soviet purchases would affect the world price, and it wouldn't matter very much where they bought the grain.

Additional Problems

1. Suppose that COMECON makes the transferable ruble convertible into Western currency and pegs the ruble to a currency composite, such as the SDR. Discuss the implications.

2. Section 9 of chapter 6 of the textbook discussed a theory of multinational enterprises. How does this theory seem to apply to the activities of large Western firms in centrally planned economies?

Answers to Self-Test

1. Council for Mutual Economic Assistance.

2. 2.5.

3. True.

4. The LDC Debt Problem

Basic Ideas

1. LDCs can be expected to be net borrowers from the DCs in normal circumstances.

2. After the oil price shocks, LDCs borrowed large sums from Western banks. Many of these funds had been deposited by oil exporters.

3. Since 1982 many LDCs have experienced difficulties in servicing their debts. There have been many crises and new lending has been sharply curtailed.

4. The large outstanding loans to LDCs with difficulties have left many banks in an exposed position.

1. Multiple choice: The country with the largest foreign debt is:
   1.1. Brazil.
   1.2. The U.S.S.R.
   1.3. Argentina.
   1.4. The United States.
   1.5. Mexico.

2. Multiple choice: Which of the following was not a major reason why the LDCs have found it difficult to service their debts?
   2.1. Recession in the DCs.
   2.2. The appreciation of the dollar in the early 1980s.
   2.3. High real interest rates.
   2.4. All of the above.
   2.5. None of the above.

Additional Problems

1. Why don't the LDCs simply refuse to pay back their debts?

2. Discuss the consequences for the United States of large-scale LDC defaults on international debt.

Answers to Self-Test

1. 1.4.

2. 2.5.

5. Review Questions

1. What are the advantages and disadvantages of economic integration, such as the formation of the EEC, for the participants and for the rest of the world?

2. Discuss international trade between centrally planned economies. Compare with trade between market economies.

3. What special problems arise in trade between market economies and centrally planned economies?

APPENDIX I — A Survey of the Pure Theory of International Trade

A.1 The National Income of a Trading Economy (Chapter 1)

Solutions to Problems from the Text

A.1.1 *Figure A.2 in the textbook was drawn by holding P_C constant and allowing P_W to vary. Derive an income curve by instead holding P_W constant and allowing P_C to vary.*

If you derive the curve properly it should resemble Figure A.2 qualitatively, with the roles of the two goods reversed. The upper and lower specialization values of P_C are P_W/c_o and P_W/w_o respectively.

A.1.2 *Equation (4) in the textbook holds for small (that is, differential) movements along the transformation curve, when both goods are being produced. What can you say about large movements? If only one good is initially produced?*

If the change in production is not infinitesimal, the left-hand side of equation (3) in the textbook could be strictly negative. Then the term in brackets in equation (4) would be negative, so that the left-hand side of that equation would be strictly less than S_C. If the economy is specialized, a change in prices does not change production, so that the term in brackets in equation (4) would still be zero.

A.2 The National Expenditure of a Trading Economy (Chapter 1)

Solutions to Problems from the Text

A.2.1 *Suppose a country has the utility function*

$$u(D_C, D_W) = D_C^{\alpha} \, D_W^{1-\alpha}$$

for some number α between zero and one. Derive a formula for $E(P_C, P_W; u)$. Verify the properties discussed in the text.

$$E(P_C, P_W; u) = \left(\frac{1}{\alpha^{\alpha}(1-\alpha)^{1-\alpha}} \right) u P_C^{\alpha} P_W^{1-\alpha}$$

A.2.2 *Derive $E(P_C, P_W; u)$ if consumers always demand wheat and cloth in equal amounts. If $u(D_C, D_W) = D_C + D_W$.*

$$E(P_C, P_W; u) = (P_C + P_W)u. \quad E(P_C, P_W; u) = min\{P_C, P_W\}u.$$

A.3 International Equilibrium (Chapter 2)

Solutions to Problems from the Text

A.3.1 *Why is it that both cloth and wheat cannot be inferior?*

Income must always equal expenditure, but if both goods were inferior, an increase in income would reduce spending on both goods, and therefore total expenditure as well.

A.3.2 *For any variables x and y, show:*

$$\left(\frac{1}{x}\right)^{\wedge} = -\hat{x}, \quad (\widehat{x \cdot y}) = \hat{x} + \hat{y},$$

and $(\widehat{x/y}) = \hat{x} - \hat{y}$.

$$\left(\frac{1}{x}\right)^{\wedge} = \frac{d(1/x)}{(1/x)} = (-1/x^2)\frac{dx}{(1/x)} = -\frac{dx}{x} = -\hat{x}$$

$$(\widehat{x \cdot y}) = \frac{d(x \cdot y)}{x \cdot y} = \frac{[y(dx) + x(dy)]}{x \cdot y} = \frac{dx}{x} + \frac{dy}{y}$$

$$= \hat{x} + \hat{y}.$$

A.3.3 *Find an explicit solution to the differential equation (DH) and use this to derive the stability condition (SC).*

Set $f(P) = M(P) - X^*(1/P)$ so that (DH) can be written: $\dot{P} = f(P)$.

Near equilibrium, this has the linear approximation:

$$\dot{P} = f'(P_o)[P(t) - P_o].$$

The solution to this linear differential equation is:

$$\dot{P} = ae^{f't} + P_o$$

where a is a parameter. It follows from this equation that $P(t)$ will converge to P_o as t goes to infinity if and only if $f' < 0$, which is the same as (SC) in the textbook.

A.3.4 *Derive the elasticity formulas for an economy with the tastes of Problem A.2.1 above and a Ricardian technology. Derive the elasticity formulas if S_C and S_W cannot be varied at all.*

If cloth is the imported good, $c = 1 - a$, $m = a$. If the economy is specialized to wheat production, $s = 0$; if both goods are being produced (that is, if the relative price is at its autarky value), s is infinite. Therefore e is infinite when P equals its autarky value and equals 1 for all other values of P.

A.4 Factor Endowments (Chapter 3)

Solutions to Problems from the Text

A.4.1 *Geometrically demonstrate exactly how an isocost curve can be derived from a given isoquant. Show how an isoquant can be derived from a given isocost curve.*

In the figure below, the curves in quadrants II and IV respectively graph $rK = 1$ and $wL = 1$. Quadrant I contains the isoquant for producing one dollar's worth of output.

To find the isocost curve corresponding to this isoquant, proceed as follows. For any point on the curve, such as A in the figure, draw a tangent. Then points B and C measure the corresponding values of $1/r$ and $1/w$ respectively. Thus D and E measure r and w, so that point F must be on the corresponding isocost curve. Repeat this procedure for each point on the isoquant to trace out the entire isocost curve. To find the isoquant corresponding to a given isocost curve, simply reverse the procedure. That is, for point F draw a tangent. Then points D' and E' measure $1/K$ and $1/L$ respectively. Thus B' and C' measure K and L, so that A is the corresponding point on the isoquant.

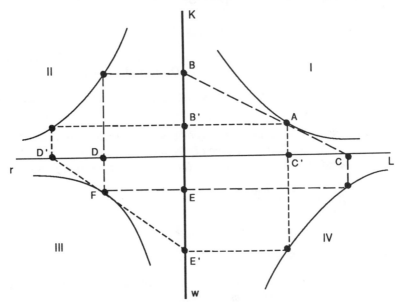

A.4.2 *Show how Figure A.11 in the textbook may alter in the presence of a factor intensity reversal. Trace out the values of S_C and S_W as K varies from zero toward infinity.*

A factor intensity reversal would raise the possibility that, in Figure A.11, there could be a second pair of intersecting K and L lines. Neither of these lines would intersect either of the first pair of lines, the second K line would intersect the second L line from above (or just the opposite of the first pair shown in the figure), and the second pair of lines would correspond to different factor prices from the first pair (but the same commodity prices).

A.4.3 *Derive the Rybczynski theorem if capital is immobile between sectors. What can you say about the factor-price equalization and Heckscher-Ohlin theorems?*

Suppose that commodity prices are held constant and that the stock of capital in the cloth sector rises. If factor prices did not change, cloth output would rise in the same proportion and wheat output would fall, as the cloth industry would attract labor from the wheat industry. This is very close to the standard Rybczynski result. But this would require that some wheat capital remain unemployed: the wheat sector has less labor but, at unchanged factor prices, uses the same capital-labor ratio as before. Thus factor prices will change if factor markets continue to clear. With the wage rising and both rentals falling, cloth output will rise in a smaller proportion than the increase in cloth capital.

A.5 Higher-Dimensional Factor-Endowments Theory* (Section 20* of Chapter 3)

Solutions to Problems from the Text

A.5.1 *Show how the presence of factor intensity reversals can alter Figure A.13 in the textbook. Discuss the implications.*

With factor intensity reversals, two isocost curves can intersect more than once.

A.5.2 *Suppose there are three goods and two factors, that all three goods are being produced in equilibrium, and that the techniques used in the three sectors relate to each other as follows:*

$$\frac{K_C}{L_C} > \frac{K_D}{L_D} > \frac{K_W}{L_W} \tag{59}$$

Now consider the price change:

$$\hat{P}_D > 0, \hat{P}_C = \hat{P}_W = 0.$$

What can you say about the consequences for factor rewards and the pattern of production?

The economy will cease producing either cloth or wheat. If it ends wheat production, the wage rises in terms of all three goods and the rent falls in terms of all three goods. If it ends cloth production, the wage falls in terms of all three goods and the rent rises in terms of all three goods.

A.5.3 *Suppose that there are three goods and two factors with relative intensities as in (59) above for all wage-rental ratios. If there are two countries, is it possible for one to specialize in deckles in equilibrium? Explain.*

If prices were such as to cause one country to specialize in deckles (the three isocost curves would not have a common intersection), the other country could not produce both cloth and wheat. Thus such a case is impossible.

A.5.4 *How does our general version of the Stolper-Samuelson theorem change if we drop the assumption that the good whose price increases uses a nonspecific assortment of factors?*

It would then be possible that an increase in the price of some commodity could cause some factor reward to rise in the same proportion, but no factor reward to rise in strictly greater proportion. In this case the favored factor's reward would still rise in terms of all goods except that whose price itself rose. Thus recipients of income from that factor would find those incomes greater in real terms, unless they just happened to spend them entirely on the good with the increased price, in which case the real incomes would be unchanged. This very minor modification is the only consequence.

A.5.5 *What can you say about the general version of the Rybczynski theorem in the case of more goods than factors if, instead of holding factor prices constant, we fix commodity prices and suppose that all factors remain fully employed?*

The Rybczynski theorem derived in the textbook ceases to apply. But, on the other hand, the duality relations (54) now apply.

A.6 Tariffs (Chapter 4)

Solutions to Problems from the Text

A.6.1 *Explicitly derive (62) in the textbook.*

$$E(q,u_t) = D_C + qD_W = [S_C + P(S_W - D_W)] + qD_W$$

$$= [S_C + q(S_W - D_W) - tP(S_W - D_W)] + qD_W$$

$$= (S_C + qS_W) + tP(D_W - S_W)$$

$$= y(q, \dots) + tPM.$$

A.6.2 *What will equation (65) in the textbook look like if we do not assume that t = 0 initially?*

$$\hat{M} = -[(c + s + m(1 - t))/(1 - mt)] \hat{P}$$
$$- [(c + s)/(1 - mt)][dt/(1 + t)].$$

A.6.3 *What does the assumption of internationally identical tastes imply about the relative sizes of $\hat{P}$ and $\hat{q}$?*

They are both positive, with the latter exceeding the former (as always) by $dt/(1 + t)$.

APPENDIX II   Sample Examinations

1. One-Hour Examinations Covering International Trade

Examination I.

1. What does it mean for an import curve to be *inelastic*? Why does it matter? Discuss some theoretical issues where elasticity is crucial, and discuss some current policy issues as well. What can you say about actual values of these elasticities?

2. SHORT ANSWER. Give only the requested answer, with no explanation or derivation.
   2.1. State the factor price equalization theorem.
   2.2. Describe the U.S. anti-dumping law.
   2.3. What is the Most-Favored-Nation clause?
   2.4. What do the following stand for: GATT, UNCTAD, OPEC, ITO?
   2.5. What is meant by "unequal exchange"?
   2.6. What is the Leontief Paradox?
   2.7. Write the optimum tariff formula.

3. In Pottstown 2 units of labor are required to produce 1 beer and 10 units of labor are required to produce one mushroom. There are 1,000 laborers in Pottstown. As all the world knows, residents of Pottstown always eat 1 mushroom with each 5 beers that they drink. Describe autarky equilibrium. What happens if Pottstown can trade with Philadelphia at the relative price of 5 beers for 3 mushrooms?

Examination II.

1. In Grafton each pumpkin requires 2 units of labor in its production and each witch requires 4 units of labor. Grafton has 400 units of labor available. In Camden 10 units of labor are required to produce each pumpkin and 5 units to produce each witch. There are 1,000 units of labor in Camden.
   1.1. Who has a comparative advantage in what? Make two equivalent statements.
   1.2. Draw production possibility frontiers for Grafton, Camden, and the world.

1.3. How do your answers to 1.2 illustrate comparative advantage? What can you predict will happen if Grafton and Camden commence free trade in pumpkins and witches?

2. Write an essay on the "New Protectionism." Be sure you discuss what it is, how it differs from the old protectionism, and what its main instruments are.

3. SHORT ANSWER. Give only the requested answer, with no explanation or derivation.
    3.1. State precisely the Rybczynski theorem.
    3.2. Draw a diagram illustrating how a tariff could reduce the domestic relative price of importables.
    3.3. Define: demand reversal; factor intensity reversal.
    3.4. Define: elasticity of import demand; elasticity of export supply; What is the algebraic relation between the two?
    3.5. Define: specific tariff; ad-valorem tariff. How does it matter which type of tariff we have?

Examination III.

1. Show geometrically that a tariff will increase the relative domestic price of importables in the tariff-levying country. Can this ever fail to happen? If so, demonstrate geometrically and explain why in words.

2. In a certain economy, an apple requires two units of land and three units of labor to produce, and a banana requires three land and two labor.
    2.1. If an apple and a banana each cost $10 in long-run competitive equilibrium, what is land's rent and labor's wage?
    2.2. Using specific numbers, illustrate the Stolper-Samuelson theorem, and explain your illustration.
    2.3. If, in the short run, factors are specific to industry, show how income distribution would instead be affected by a price change, and compare with your answer in 2.2.

3. SHORT ANSWER. Give only the requested answer, with no justification or explanation.
    3.1. State the Marshall-Lerner condition.
    3.2. What does it mean for a transfer to be "undereffected"? What is its "secondary burden"?
    3.3. State Walras's Law.
    3.4. What is a "beggar-my-neighbor" policy?
    3.5. Define: MRT, MRS, MRTS.

Examination IV.

1. Briefly describe the salient features of international trade between and among the developed countries of the world, as a group, and the less

developed countries. Show how the theoretical principles developed in this course can be used to explain various characteristics of this trade. Are there any respects in which the theory is deficient for this purpose?

2. "Nearly all valid arguments for a tariff are second-best arguments." Discuss.

3. Discuss the transfer problem. Be sure your discussion touches on: the classical presumption, secondary burden, an undereffected transfer. How would your discussion change if the Marshall-Lerner condition did not hold?

2. One-Hour Examinations Covering International Monetary Economics

Examination V.

1. Describe the process of international adjustment under a gold exchange standard. Include in your discussion an evaluation of the advantages and disadvantages of the system with reference to historical performance.

2. What is meant by Purchasing Power Parity? Exactly what roles does it play in international adjustment? Describe any relevant empirical evidence.

3. SHORT ANSWER. Give only the requested answer, with no justification or explanation.
   3.1. Define: perfect international capital mobility.
   3.2. What are the "Rules of the Game"?
   3.3. Suppose that the spot price of a U.K. pound in New York is $2.00/£, the three-month forward rate is $1.96/£, the interest rate on U.S. Treasury bills is 10 percent per annum, and the interest rate on U.K. Treasury bills is 14 percent per annum. Describe the interest arbitrage that would likely result.
   3.4. What are Eurodollars? About how many are there?
   3.5. What does it mean for the foreign-exchange market to be efficient?
   3.6. Draw import curves for two countries and illustrate a case where the country with the higher APM has the lower MPM.
   3.7. What is sterilization and what is its purpose?
   3.8. Describe present exchange-rate arrangements.

Examination VI.

1. Suppose that France is specialized in wine production and Germany in machine production, and that the equilibrium terms of trade are two units of wine per machine. The following data apply:

	France	Germany
Constant Output	100 W	50 Ma
Velocity of Circulation	1	1
Price Elasticity of Imports	1/2	1
Marginal Propensity to Import	1/4	1/2
Monetary Unit (gold)	fr1=1 oz.	DM1=2 oz.

1.1. If the world stock of gold is 1,000 ounces, what are the equilibrium price levels and money stocks?

1.2. If France finds an additional 500 ounces of gold, what is the new equilibrium? Qualitatively describe the process of adjustment.

1.3. How would your answer to 1.2 change if the French marginal propensity to import were instead 3/4?

2. "In many ways the Bretton Woods international monetary system was designed in response to real or imagined lessons of experience before and after the First World War." Discuss this statement.

3. Write an essay on the covered interest parity theory of the forward exchange rate.

Examination VII.

1. Discuss the relative efficacy of monetary and fiscal policy for domestic stabilization purposes in an open economy.

2. Describe the mechanics of multiple deposit creation in the Eurodollar market.

3. Write a short essay on the "dilemma" of the gold exchange standard.

4. Discuss the forces that would tend to correct automatically an imbalance of payments of a country which maintained a fixed exchange rate and which was too small appreciably to influence world prices.

Examination VIII.

1. What is sterilization and what is its purpose? What limits it? Is it common?

2. In America, the money supply is $400, $k = 1$, and real GNP consists of 400 bushels of wheat. In Europe, the money supply = fr800, the velocity of money is 1/2, and real GNP consists of 100 barrels of wine. The terms of trade are one barrel of wine per bushel of wheat, and the American exchange rate $R = \$1/\text{fr}$.

2.1. If America and Europe maintain a fixed exchange rate, what cumulative payments imbalance is necessary to establish equilibrium? What are the equilibrium price levels?

2.2. Suppose that instead America and Europe maintain their initial money supplies and allow their exchange rate to float. How must it change in order to establish equilibrium?

3. SHORT ANSWER. Write only the requested answer, with no explanation or justification.

   3.1. Write the formula for Purchasing Power Parity.

   3.2. What special role did the dollar play in the Bretton Woods system?

   3.3. What were the Smithsonian Agreement, the Rambouillet meeting, and the Second Amendment to the IMF Articles of Agreement?

   3.4. EMS stands for:
      (a) Export Mobilization System.
      (b) Eastern Magical Snake.
      (c) European Monetary Scale.
      (d) European Monetary System.
      (e) None of the above.

   3.5. The balance of trade deficit can be thought of as:
      (a) Insoluble.
      (b) The excess of exports over imports.
      (c) The excess of income over absorption.
      (d) The excess of absorption over exorption.
      (e) None of the above.

3. Two-Hour Examinations Covering International Economics

Examination IX.

1. The rapid growth of the international economy since the Second World War has been a recurring theme of this course. Briefly describe the nature of this growth. Discuss its implications, using the theory developed in the course.

2. Sharp fluctuations of exchange rates have taken place with some frequency since the adoption of managed floating by major industrial nations. Discuss in terms of the theory developed in this course.

3. Write an essay on the optimum tariff. Make sure that your discussion includes: an analysis of the optimum tariff, the relation between the optimum tariff and the revenue-maximizing tariff, welfare implications, and the relevance of this to actual experience.

4. SHORT ANSWER. Give only the requested answer, without explanation or derivation.

4.1. What does OECD stand for?

4.2. What are the "Rules of the Game"?

4.3. Show in a diagram the effects on the forward exchange rate of a fall in the foreign interest rate.

4.4. What is the effective rate of protection? Give a formula.

4.5. Define: gold exchange standard, adjustable peg, managed floating.

Examination X.

1. The degree of international capital mobility has played an important role in the analysis of international economic phenomena at several points in this course. What is meant by the degree of international capital mobility; is there more than one meaning? Mention and briefly discuss several issues where it is important. What can you say about the degree of capital mobility in the world economy since the Second World War?

2. In Europe cloth production requires 10 labor per unit and food production requires 5 labor per unit, whereas in Asia cloth requires 30 labor and food 20 labor. The European labor force equals 300 and the Asian 3,000. Europe always spends two-thirds of its income on cloth and Asia always spends one-half of its income on cloth. The world money supply consists of 4,200 identical gold coins. In each country $k = 1$. Find the complete world equilibrium. Draw all relevant diagrams ($PPFs$, import curves, etc.) and find the magnitudes of all economic variables (prices, quantities traded, money supplies, etc.).

3. SHORT ANSWER. Give a short, direct answer to each question, without justification or derivation.

3.1. Define a gold exchange standard.

3.2. Define ad-valorem and specific tariffs.

3.3. Has it ever mattered whether tariffs were ad-valorem or specific? When?

3.4. What are the short-run consequences of a tariff for domestic income distribution?

3.5. What are the long-run consequences of a tariff for domestic income distribution?

3.6. Describe current exchange-rate arrangements in the world.

3.7. Write the formula for an optimum tariff in terms of export supply elasticities.

3.8. Define "Purchasing Power Parity" and "interest parity."

3.9. What does it mean for a transfer to be "overeffected" or "undereffected"? When will one or the other happen?

Examination XI.

1. Write an essay on the principle of comparative advantage. Be sure to include a precise statement of the principle in its most general form.

2. What are multinational enterprises, why do they exist, and where are they located?

3. Discuss the relative merits of fixed and floating exchange rates.

4. SHORT ANSWER. Give only the requested answer, without explanation or derivation.
   4.1. What is the "Eurodollar carousel"?
   4.2. What does it mean for foreign exchange markets to be efficient?
   4.3. Why is it difficult to determine whether the foreign exchange markets are efficient or not?
   4.4. Define: income elasticity of import demand.
   4.5. What is the Leontief Paradox?
   4.6. Describe covered interest arbitrage.
   4.7. What is sterilization? offset?
   4.8. What is meant by "unequal exchange"?
   4.9. Define: countervailing duties. Describe the pertinent U.S. law.
   4.10. Briefly describe the role of the LDCs in the present international monetary system.

Examination XII.

1. Write an essay on U.S. trade policy since the Second World War. Be sure to include a discussion of the Tokyo Round and of the "new protectionism."

2. State and prove the Rybczynski theorem.

3. Write an essay on international migration.

4. There are two distinct theories which purport to explain the forward premium. Briefly describe each of these theories. Which of the two seems to offer a better explanation? Can the two be made consistent with each other?

Examination XIII.

1. Discuss the principle of *comparative advantage*. Be sure you define the principle, explain what it implies, and discuss its relevance to the world in which we live. How general is it?

2. In America, the money supply is $800, $k = 1$, and real GNP consists of 400 bushels of wheat. In Europe, the money supply = fr800, $k = 2$, and real GNP consists of 100 barrels of wine. The terms of trade are one barrel of wine per bushel of wheat, and the American exchange rate $R = \$2/\text{fr}$.

   2.1. If America and Europe maintain a fixed exchange rate, what cumulative payments imbalance is necessary to establish equilibrium? What are the equilibrium price levels?

   2.2. Suppose that instead America and Europe maintain their initial money supplies and allow their exchange rate to float. How must it change in order to establish equilibrium?

3. SHORT ANSWER. Give only the requested answer, with no explanation or justification.

   3.1. Define: intra-industry trade.

   3.2. Distinguish between national and international returns to scale.

   3.3. Briefly describe proposed changes to current U.S. immigration law.

   3.4. Write the formula for covered interest parity.

   3.5. Write the formula for Purchasing Power Parity.

   3.6. Describe the U.S. countervailing duty law.

   3.7. State the Rybczynski theorem in precise form.

   3.8. What is a dual exchange market? Cite an actual example.

   3.9. Describe the present international monetary system.

   3.10. What is forward exchange?

4. When does a tariff on imports raise the relative domestic price of imports? Prove that your answer is correct.